150 Activities *for* BORED DOGS

150 Activities *for* BORED DOGS

Surefire Ways to Keep Your Dog Active and Happy

Sue Owens Wright

Adams Media
Avon, Massachusetts

Published by Adams Media, an F+W Publications Company
57 Littlefield Street, Avon, MA 02322. U.S.A.
www.adamsmedia.com

ISBN 10: 1-59337-688-X
ISBN 13: 978-1-59337-688-8

Printed in Canada.
J I H G F E D C B A

Library of Congress Cataloging-in-Publication Data
Wright, Sue Owens.
150 activities for bored dogs / Sue Owens Wright
p. cm.
ISBN-13: 978-1-59337-688-8
ISBN-10: 1-59337-688-X
1. Games for dogs. I.Title. II.Title: One hundred fifty activities for bored dogs.
SF427.45.W75 2007
636.7'0887—dc22 2006102186

Interior art: Part 1 photograph © iStockphoto.com/pederk, Part 2 photograph © iStockphoto.com/JoopS, Jack Russell Terrier © iStockphoto.com/Shorrocks, tennis ball © iStockphoto.com/pjmorley, and dog silhouette © iStockphoto.com/Pixel-Pi

DEDICATION

In loving memory of Daisy, 1995–2006.
"I'll give you a daisy a day, dear."

ACKNOWLEDGMENTS

Heartfelt gratitude to my agent, editors, and everyone who contributed their dogs' favorite activities. With their help, this book was written for all the dogs we love that need no one to teach them how to enrich our lives in countless ways.

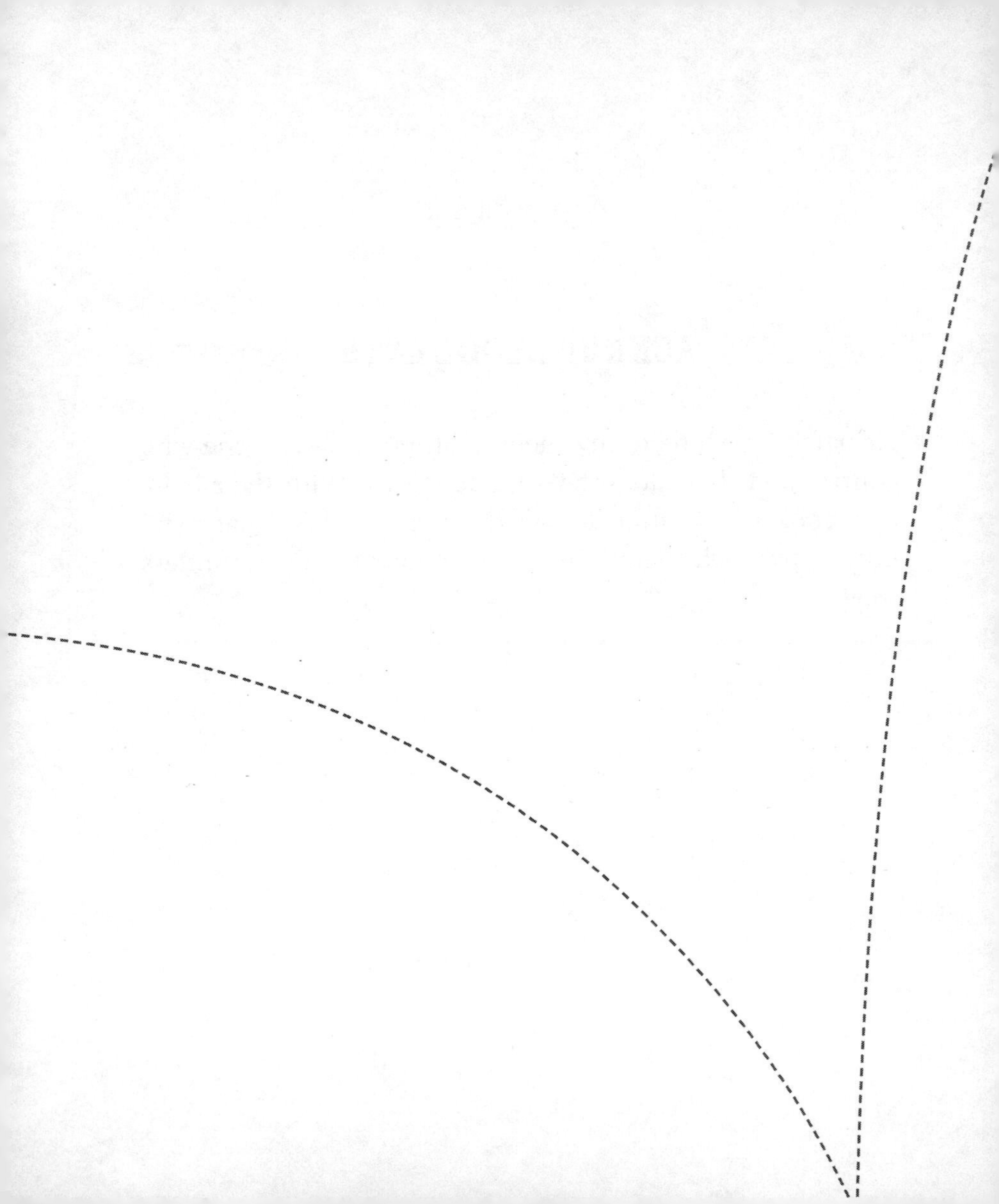

CONTENTS

PART 1

It's a Dog's Life

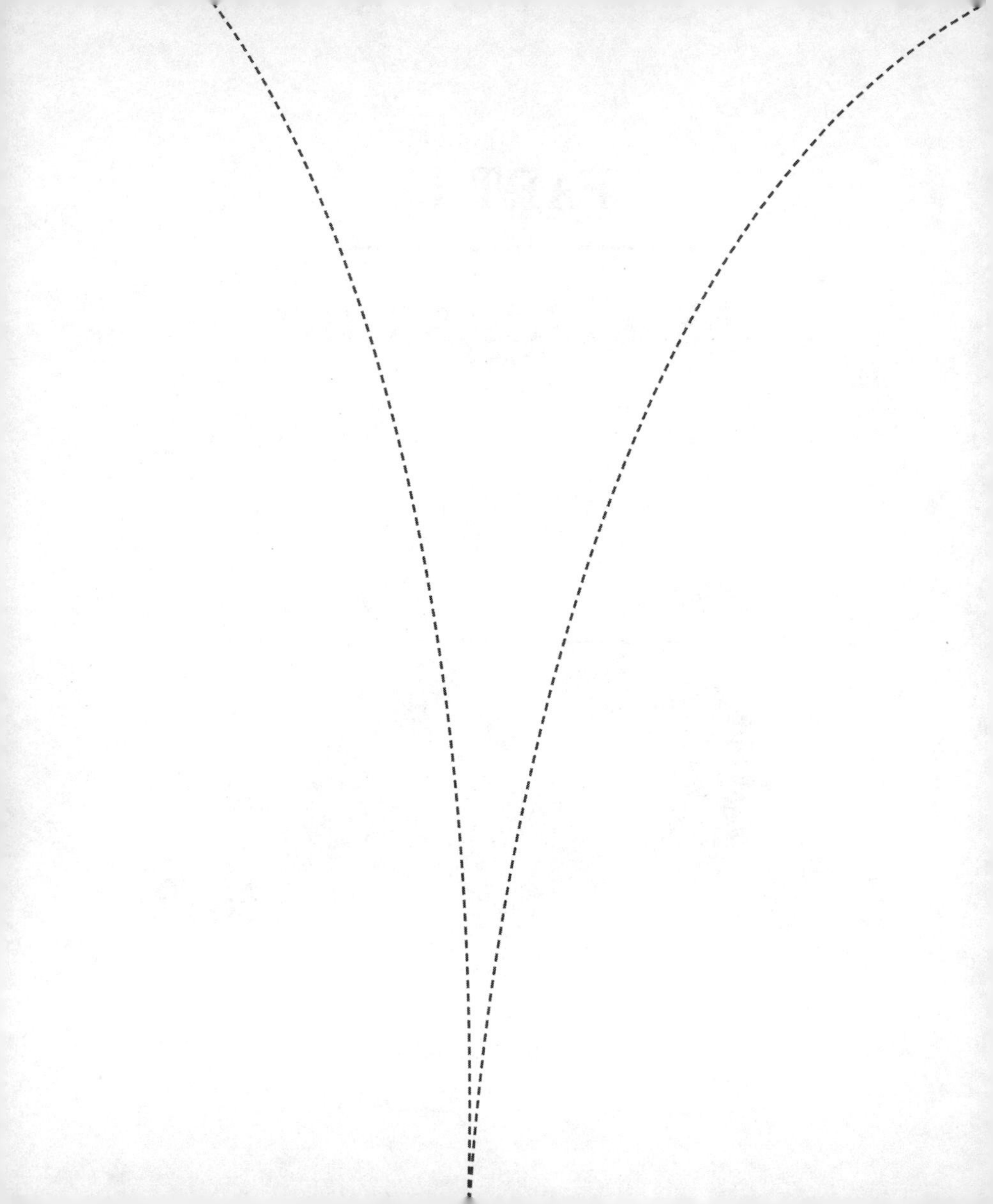

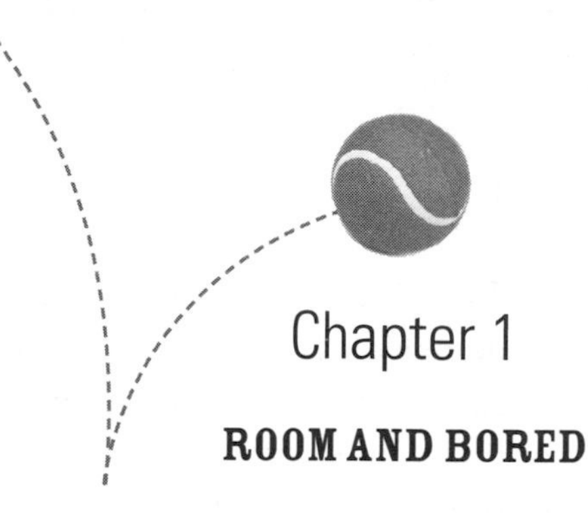

Chapter 1

ROOM AND BORED

Here's a public service announcement you probably haven't heard on TV: Do you know where your dog is right now? Do you know what he's doing? While he's probably not out street racing or hanging with Snoop Dogg, he may still be getting into his own special brand of doggie mischief when you aren't around. If Fido's an outdoor dog, you probably don't need to aerate your lawn or plow the garden—your bored dog will do it for you. If you have an indoor dog, Habitat for Humanity might have to rebuild your home in the wake of Hurricane Hound.

Why does your dog sometimes morph into a Tasmanian devil in your absence? It's because he's lonely and bored, bored, bored. This book explores why it's important to keep a dog happy when he can't have your full attention and offers suggestions on how to do it, many of them from dog owners like you. You might come up with some ideas of your own along the way.

Demolition Doggie

You might wonder why your dog should be bored. He may have the whole backyard to himself; he may have an entire acre to himself. The problem is that you aren't in it. I know of one such dog that chewed the siding off a house, and stories like that aren't unusual. If a dog is left on his own for long stretches of time, he'll find inventive and often destructive ways to entertain himself.

Compared to the offspring of some other species, puppies stay with their dams for a very short time—sometimes as little as six weeks. We separate them from their mothers and the companionship of their littermates, and once the cuteness of puppyhood is past, too often the dog is relegated to a lonely life.

Dogs are pack animals—they like to be with other dogs. If you only have one dog, you and your family are the other members of your dog's pack. He looks to you for companionship and attention. If he doesn't get it, that drives him a little crazy. If you were in solitary confinement day in and day out, you'd go crazy, too.

Sure, someone has to work to bring home the Bacon Beggin' Strips. But unless you work part-time or out of your home, your dog has to handle a lot of alone time: eight hours a day, five days a week. I won't get on my doggie soapbox and lecture about why people who work full-time jobs shouldn't have dogs unless every day at the workplace is Bring Your Dog to Work Day. Suffice to say that this could be the origin of the saying "It's a dog's life."

Sofa's Choice

You've no doubt seen one of the most common remnants of Lonely Dog décor—the shredded sofa. You may even have owned one of these Shaggy Chic items yourself. My parents sacrificed their designer leather sofa to two rescued Scottish terriers that mistook it for a very expensive chew toy. As with many rescues, Laddie and Duffy needed time to settle into their cushy new life with my parents. Lots of time! Unfortunately, every time Mom and Dad left the house, even for a little while, their two holy terriers began to tear into the sofa with a vengeance.

Sofas aren't the only victims of the frustrated, lonely dog. Anything in the house is fair game, and the more expensive, the better. Among other highly prized targets of demolition doggies are fashion accessories like purses and shoes; necessities like socks and underwear; electronics such as phones, computers, and vacuum cleaner cords; and that classic snack, the sampler tray (otherwise known as the kitty litter box).

Diamonds Aren't a Dog's Best Friend

Left to their own devices, lonely dogs have been known to gnaw furniture legs, shred pillows, or, if all else fails, chase their tails until they're too dizzy to care. My dog was a little different. Daisy was a jewel thief.

My earrings began to disappear soon after I adopted my basset hound Daisy, but I didn't make the connection right away. At first, I suspected the housekeeper. But when the jewelry continued to disappear long after she stopped cleaning my house, I was stumped.

Then one morning I made a discovery in Daisy's dog basket: one of my diamond earrings, slightly gnawed, with the other nowhere in sight. Since she wasn't wearing the earrings, I concluded she was eating them and took her to the vet. The X-rays looked normal, no diamond earrings or tiaras in sight, and that left but one conclusion—one so nasty that even Sherlock Holmes would have hesitated to investigate it.

Sure enough, one sunny morning I noticed that Daisy's "lawn fertilizer" was glinting in an unnatural manner. I'll spare you the details involved in retrieving my booty. Let's just say that after my jewelry was cleaned and thoroughly sanitized, it was as good as new. Once again, I had all my pairs of earrings matched and displayed in my jewelry chest, and until now no one has been the wiser.

When we adopted our other basset, Bubba Gump, Daisy finally had a constant companion to entertain her whenever I wasn't around. She soon lost her taste for expensive jewelry, and the Case of the Canine Kleptomaniac was officially closed.

Whether a dog displays a preference for Henredon or Harry Winston, her destructive behavior in her owner's absence can be costly. In many cases, it costs the dog her chance at a happy home. Whether your new charge is a puppy or an older dog, it's important to find constructive ways to keep her entertained in your absence and preserve your home and belongings as well as your peace of mind.

The Backyard Blues—It's Enough to Make a Dog Howl!

In any suburban neighborhood, you hear the sounds of lonely dogs singing the noontime backyard blues. Well, they aren't exactly singing. They're yipping, barking, howling, and making a noisy nuisance of themselves, at least to any neighbors who must endure the din. Maybe your neighbor has small children who nap in the afternoons, or maybe he works nights and sleeps during the day (or tries to). Even dog lovers can tolerate only so much of that racket before making complaints. While you're at work, oblivious to the trouble brewing in your own backyard, your neighbor is probably cursing, stuffing his ears with cotton balls, and plotting ways to get even with you and your four-legged nuisance.

Sometimes those ways can be harmful to the dog, as in the case of the person who poisoned his neighbor's Labrador retrievers because of their constant barking. This is an extreme and thankfully rare reaction to a pet nuisance problem. Still, if you've ever lived next door to a barkaholic bowser, you understand how frustrating and irritating the ceaseless cacophony can be. Fortunately, both of the dogs survived.

If you leave your dog alone in your backyard for hours at a time, he may be barking a blue streak, too. What else is there for him to do all day but bark at squirrels, the postman, ants, or whatever else happens to wander into his territory? He's just doing his job. A dog is hard-wired to think his primary directive is to guard your property in your absence. You can't blame a dog for following his instincts. But you can blame his owner for not making sure he isn't annoying the neighbors while his owner is away.

The Chain Gang

The only thing sadder than the lonely backyard dog is the lonely backyard dog at the end of a chain. Being left alone all day in the yard is punishment enough for a highly social creature like the dog. Shackling him in chains is even worse. In Elizabethan times, it was common to see dogs chained at the entrances of castles or manor houses to guard the inhabitants and ward off potential enemies. Queen Elizabeth II might not chain her corgis at the gates of Buckingham Palace to discourage the paparazzi, but it's amazing how many other people still think it's fine to leave a dog chained in the backyard—as though that were any kind of life for man's best friend.

A watch belongs on a chain, but no matter how long the chain, a watchdog does not. Dogs can quickly tangle themselves around trees or posts so completely that they can't unwind themselves or even turn around. If they can't reach their food or water, they might go hungry or, if the day is hot, suffer fatal consequences. Dogs can even strangle while trying to free themselves from their backyard bondage. In the case of a natural disaster, dogs left chained can be seriously injured or worse. Animal rescuers discovered dogs in the aftermath of Hurricane Katrina that were still tethered at the end of a chain. Many had drowned because they could not escape the rising waters. Fortunately, some cities have implemented laws that make it illegal to chain a dog. Chained dogs can become aggressive and are more liable to attack a child or anyone who might wander too close.

Dogs aren't burglar alarms. Burglar alarms don't need their owners around to give them love and attention. Bottom line: If your dog is at the end of any kind of restraint, you should always be at the other end of it.

Only the Lonely

If your dog placed an ad in the personals column of your local newspaper, it might read something like this: "SB& WNM (Single Black & White Neutered Male), 28 (3 in dog years). Sincere, intelligent, handsome dog looking for lifelong companion to share fun, frolic, and long walks. Likes to stop and smell the roses and anything else that needs smelling."

Unfortunately, there's no Lonely Hearts Club for dogs. They can't place ads in the paper for a playmate, but they would if they could. Dogs prefer to hang out with the pack, a behavioral remnant of their wolf ancestry that hasn't been diminished by their long-term association with humans. Embedded somewhere deep in the recesses of a dog's brain is the memory of what can happen to a lone wolf.

In the wild, wolves live and hunt in groups. According to Stephen Budiansky, author of *The Truth about Dogs,* they are better able to defend their territories and obtain more food by cooperating with other wolves within a strict hierarchical society: "Wolves that hunt very large prey such as moose may form packs with as many as twenty to thirty members, but even when the food supply consists of smaller game, cooperative hunting by smaller packs of four to seven brings in more food than the sum of those four to seven wolves operating on their own could manage." Of course, wolf packs of that size range over hundreds of miles of wilderness, not a fraction of an acre in suburbia, as does your domesticated canine, who would be more inclined to hunt a mouse than a moose. What would a shih tzu do with a moose, anyway?

If you want to see the real spirit of democracy in action, don't look to Washington, D.C. Instead, observe the social interactions of a wolf pack. Here, Budiansky says, you'll see the concepts of give and take, cooperation, cohesiveness, and adaptation in action. Rules within the pack are strictly enforced because they ensure the survival of the group and the vigor of their progeny, which are always the issue of alphas, the strongest members of the pack. Although the lone wolf does occasionally exist in the wild, a wolf on his own doesn't have nearly as great a chance of survival as do wolves living in groups.

This pack mentality is also a primary factor in dog boredom. Domestic dogs are highly social animals that need company, whether it is a person or another animal. In the absence of companionship, your dog needs some form of engaging entertainment to distract her from the fact that she's alone and to keep her from becoming a demolition doggie. That's where you come in.

Some breeds of dogs are more pack oriented than others. Breeds that typically hunt cooperatively, such as beagles and basset hounds, may be more discontent with living the single life than some other less gregarious breeds. I have observed this in my own dogs. When I first adopted my basset hound Daisy, I noticed that she went a little berserk when I left her alone for any period of time. After I adopted my second basset, Bubba Gump, that behavior changed for the better. Daisy was much more contented having another dog around—just as soon, at least, as Bubba was clear on who was Top Dog around our house.

The Truth About Cats and Dogs

Sometimes dogs aren't all that particular about the company they keep. If it's a choice between complete solitude and a companion of another species, dogs can be quite content around any kind of pet, even a cat! I discovered this with my first basset. Butterscotch was an only dog and a dyed-in-the-fur cat hater until Tabby adopted us. Not only did Butter accept Tabby into her territory (no other cat dared set a paw in her yard), but they eventually even shared a bed. Sleeping with a cat was something I never thought I'd see Butter do.

Dogs have also been known to adapt to the company of other kinds of animals. Even a turtle can be a good companion for a dog. There have been many instances of dogs making fast friends with animals that usually run fast when chased, such as rabbits, raccoons, and squirrels. (Of course, if your dog is anything like my Daisy, you probably wouldn't want to consider a squirrel as her backyard buddy since she probably already acts pretty doggone nutty.)

Dogs Gone Wild

Sometimes dogs go wild, but it doesn't have anything to do with letting loose on spring break or flashing the crowd at

Mardi Gras. It's called separation anxiety. You've probably seen footage like that on Animal Planet that shows exactly what happens when the owner of a dog like this leaves the house or even, in some cases, merely steps outside the room. Pandemonium ensues. The dog barks and howls, scratches furiously at the door, jumps up on the furniture, rips the sofa, tears down the Venetian blinds, chews everything chewable, and strews garbage all over the place. Some dogs have even been known to crash right through plate glass windows. You come home at the end of the day to find that the place looks like the aftermath of a frat party.

Some owners actually set the stage for this destructive behavior by giving their pets too much attention when they are around the house. When they leave, their dogs suffer a meltdown. Suddenly no one's around to constantly entertain and spoil them in the manner to which they've become accustomed.

While many dogs, by nature, are usually content to lie around the house resting while their owners are gone, even normally well-behaved dogs can become home-wreckers if they are bored enough. Stephen Budiansky believes that this "high anxiety" is usually the result of boredom from being left home alone for too long with not enough doggie activities for entertainment. Dogs like to run, chew, and dig, and they can't do that very effectively if they are shut up in the house all day long.

If you can't be with your dog all day or provide your dog with the much-needed companionship that he craves, make sure you provide stimulation for him in other ways or you may return to a real Animal House.

No dog is an island. Dogs are like humans in that they need a certain amount of social interaction with their own kind. Of course, what they want most is to be with you, the sole object of their affection.

"Some destructive dogs are genuinely hyperactive," Budiansky explains. "That is, they have a truly abnormal condition." He explains that those dogs have lower levels of endorphins, nature's feel-good opiates that are produced in the brain. Long-distance runners and athletes know all about endorphins. Dogs have them, too, and like us they need to be physically active in order to get their endorphin level high. When under stress, endorphin-deficient dogs will engage in activities that may be destructive to your home but are constructive for the dog because they help stimulate the production of the needed hormone to relieve their anxiety.

Some dogs may need medical help for their chemical imbalance, in which case your veterinarian may prescribe Puppy Prozac.

Crate and Barrel

A crate can be a great training tool when used properly. It can be effective for house-training and to serve as the dog's home within a home. The crate is a must for your dog's safety when traveling by plane, train, or automobile. It can also be a haven of security for your dog. But for some dogs, whose owners leave them shut up in it all day long, it becomes a prison. The crate must never be used for punishment, or your dog may eventually refuse to set a paw in it.

Your dog can't mess the house or get into trouble if she's confined to her crate when you're not around to supervise. That's fine for a few hours at a stretch, and it's even good for your dog to have some alone time to learn to entertain herself with her toys and chews. However, leaving a dog confined in a crate for eight to ten hours a day is not only unkind, it's also counterproductive to housetraining. Dogs don't like to soil their sleeping area. Would you? Even a prison cell has a toilet, and for long-term confinement, a dog should have access to potty privileges.

In her book *Dog-Friendly Dog Training,* Andrea Arden recommends these ways of confining a dog to an area but allowing for the call of nature:

- A bathroom gated off with a baby gate.
- An exercise pen.
- An exercise pen including a crate. In this case, the crate is the dog's bedroom, and the dog's toilet is in the area sectioned off by the pen.
- A crate connected to a doggie door that leads to a safely enclosed dog run. This option also helps the dog housetrain himself while you're gone.

Any well-trained dog will try his best to hold it the whole time you're gone, but no dog has a bladder *that* big. So, if you've ever wondered why your dog barrels out of his crate each night when you come home from work, it may not be just because he's overjoyed to see you. He's got to go see a dog about a man.

Do You Have the Wrong Dog?

Finding the right dog is almost as difficult as finding Mr. or Mrs. Right. When you realize that your relationship with a dog is likely to last longer than many marriages, the choice becomes even more important. A dog that is mismatched to your personality and lifestyle can influence your life as terribly as the wrong mate. And just as many prospective dog owners succumb to an adorable puppy as those who fall for a pretty face and make an emotional decision instead of an informed, intelligent one.

Size Matters

Too many people end up with the wrong dog, which is the main reason so many dogs end up in shelters. Once that cute little puppy grows into those Number Nine paws, people realize they are in way over their heads. You can take that statement literally if you have an Irish wolfhound—upright on hind legs, a full-grown wolfhound stands over six feet tall. People may have neither the space for a 100-pound dog nor the ability to afford to keep it in kibble. The dog may also be too much for them to handle. That much dog at the end of a leash requires someone at the other end who weighs at least as much and can let the dog know who's boss.

I met a woman with an aging, blind Lhasa apso who felt she needed to get a watchdog. Since her dog was deaf and nearly blind, naturally it didn't bark much. The woman was tiny, ninety pounds if an ounce, but she wanted a rottweiler or something just as big for protection—this though she could barely control her Lhasa! As I sat listening, I thought, "Well, here's another doggie disaster in the making, and it's the dog that will suffer the most." I tried to convince her that a smaller dog can be every bit as good a watchdog as a large dog and is much easier to control. To a burglar, a small dog sounds much bigger than he is. Actually, the barking of any dog is a deterrent to crime because it alerts you and others to trouble.

Before you choose a dog, it's important to know how big the dog will be when full grown, what its temperament and activity level are like, and other factors. Are you athletic and always on the move, or are you more of a couch spud who doesn't budge from the same spot for hours? Some breeds are highly energetic and require a lot of activity for optimum health and happiness. Choose a dog according to your work habits, your personality, and the space you live in.

Other Considerations

According to the Program for Companion Animal Behavior at the UC Davis School of Veterinary Medicine, there are some important questions you should ask yourself before you bring a dog into your home:

1. **Are you really a dog person?** Consider your past experiences with animals. If you were brought up in a household filled with cats, birds, or other species, you may not be prepared to take on the greater demands of dog ownership. A dog requires a lot more of your time, attention, and energy than a fish or a hamster, and this commitment can last a decade or more.
2. **Why are you considering a dog for a pet?**
3. **Do you have the space at your residence to comfortably house a dog?**
4. **Can you afford to keep a dog?** Dogs can be expensive. Some breeds have more medical problems than others, as do aging dogs, which is why so many senior pets end up in shelters. I've spent thousands of dollars on my dogs for various medical problems.

Once you've determined that you do want a dog, it's time to decide what kind of dog you want. The UC Davis program advises you to make this decision by deciding which of the following characteristics you're most looking for in a dog:

- Quiet companionship
- Low maintenance

- Well behaved
- Entertaining
- Good playmate for children
- Athletic, high endurance (necessary for a jogging partner)
- Working ability (such as a herding dog or a retriever)
- Protective, aggressive (necessary for a guard dog)

Another important consideration, and the primary focus of this book, is whether you can accommodate the dog's needs during your vacations and absences. You can't just pick up and leave home any time you want when you have a dog. You need to make proper arrangements for your pet while you are away.

Fight Fido Fads

It can be confusing trying to choose just the right dog from all the breeds out there. Do your research before you commit to a certain breed. People have a tendency to follow fads, not only in attire but also in pets. They see a celebrity or a movie with a certain breed of dog and immediately want the same kind of dog, even though that breed may be all wrong for them. In addition, the high demand leads unscrupulous people to enter the dog-breeding business to try to turn a quick buck—the dogs they sell are rarely screened for genetic problems and are almost always inferior examples of the breed.

One reliable source to consult for breed information is The Complete Dog Book, *published by the American Kennel Club (AKC). The book lists every breed recognized by the AKC and provides important details about each one.*

An example of this is the Disney Dalmatian disaster. After *101 Dalmatians* was first released in 1961, parents went out in droves to buy Dalmatian puppies for their children. Few knew that these beautiful black-and-white spotted dogs were high-energy working animals originally bred to run alongside coaches. By the same token, all those parents who bought their kids a St. Bernard after seeing the movie *Beethoven* probably weren't prepared to spend so much on dog food—not to mention the showers of dog spit a St. Bernard produces every time it shakes. When it comes to owning a dog that slobbers a lot, neat freaks need not apply.

Mixed-breed dogs make great pets. They generally have fewer health problems and live longer than purebred dogs, and they'll love you just as much as any purebred—perhaps even more. There are always plenty of mutts at the local shelter, just waiting to be rescued.

Taking time to educate yourself and make an informed decision about the dog you are planning to bring into your life can save you a lot of grief and disappointment. It will also ensure that the dog you choose will be the best dog for you and that you will be the kind of owner who is best for the dog.

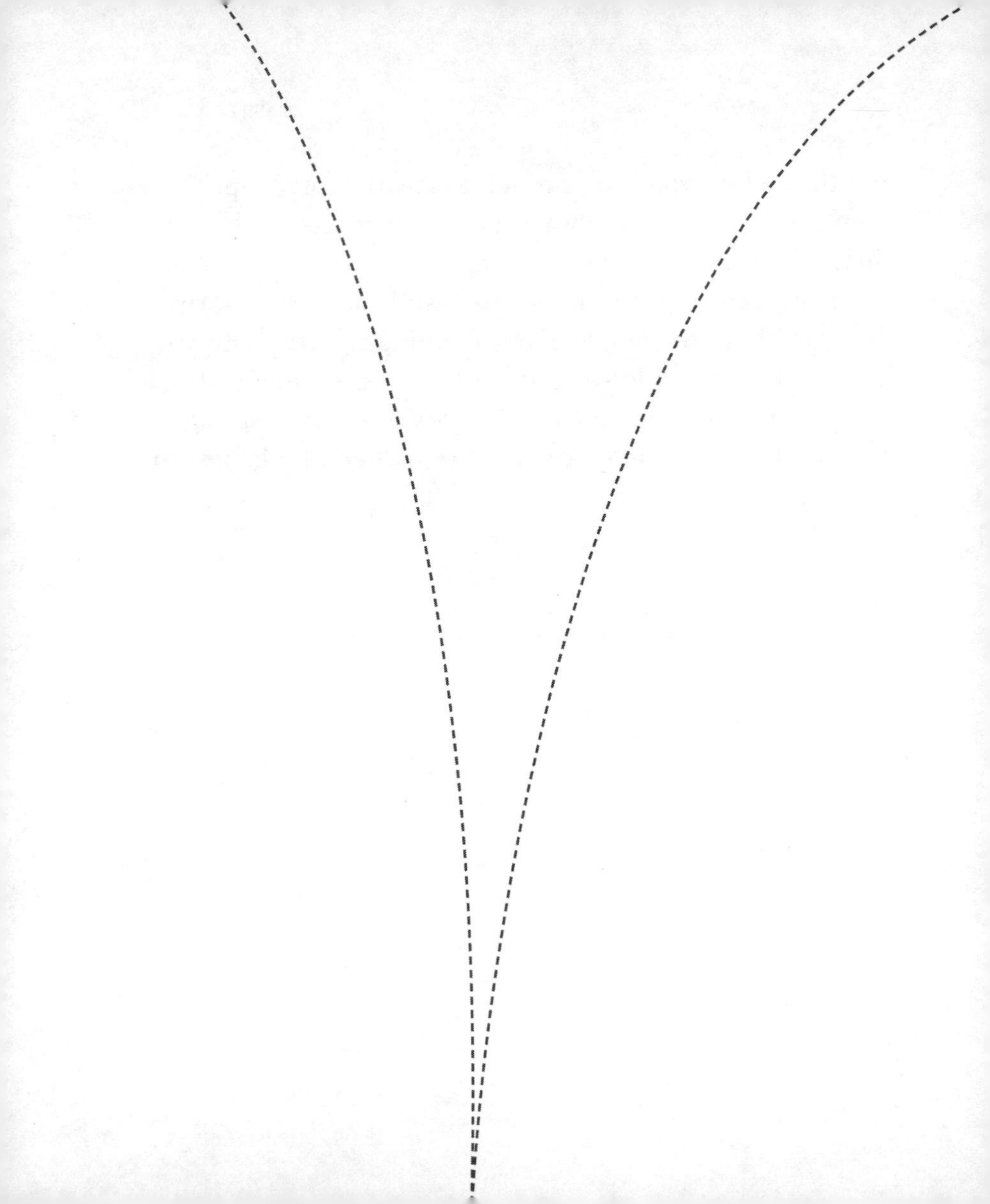

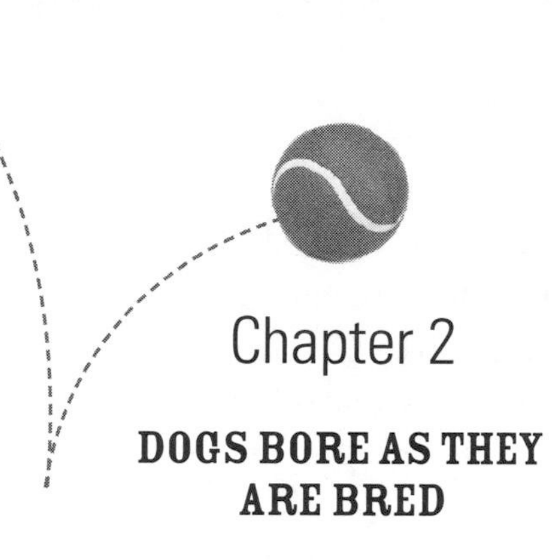

Chapter 2

DOGS BORE AS THEY ARE BRED

To understand what makes a dog a dog, you need to look back a few thousand millennia. Even in prehistoric times, when man was still dragging his knuckles in the dirt, canines were establishing their status as pets.

Heir of the Dog

It's around 100,000 B.D.C. (Before Domesticated Canines). Og and his wife are sitting around the campfire gnawing on a juicy pterodactyl drumstick when suddenly they become aware of a pair of eyes glowing in the darkness outside their cave. Og is just about to lob his spear at the intruder when he sees that it's not a saber-toothed tiger or a raptor—it's the new canid that's been roaming the Neanderthal's bedrock community. Though this creature looks a lot like a wolf, it's not. The animal is not as afraid of humans as wolves are, so it doesn't run away when Og grunts a few threats at it. This furry fellow is looking for a meal all right, but unlike the wolf, he's more interested in what Og's eating than in eating Og. The dog begs and gives Og that pleading look humans find so irresistible. Og takes pity, tosses the intruder a scrap of meat, and the handwriting is on the cave wall. Og now has a dog.

Dogs began their association with man not as predators but as scavengers. That relationship still exists. Humans were as busy trashing the planet in prehistoric times as they are today. Then as now, anywhere you found *Homo sapiens*, you'd find a garbage dump, and that's the main reason *Canis familiaris* first chose to become so familiar with mankind. Why knock yourself out chasing down game, risking life and limb for a hit-or-miss meal, when there's a primordial picnic ripe for the taking down at Og's place? As this opportunistic canine cleans the last scraps of smoked pterodactyl meat from the drumstick Og's wife has tossed out on the compost pile, he's no doubt thinking, "Mmmm. This is the Og's dinner."

The first fossil evidence that establishes our close relationship with the canine is from about twelve thousand years ago. Archaeologists discovered a burial site in Israel dating to this time that contained an old man cradling a puppy in his hand. No matter the reason for their burial together, it seems clear that there was a strong connection between man and dog. By this time human beings have evolved beyond the hunting, gathering, and grunting stage and are now farmers, raising crops and livestock in an agricultural society. The dog has evolved quite a lot, too, over time. He now looks more like a modern-day wolf than his wolf ancestors did. He is smaller in size, has different physical features, and his coat is mottled in color. Man and dog were living and working together, and the very survival of the two species was intertwined. Dogs had become our domestic helpers and protectors, and in return we fed and sheltered the dogs. From this symbiotic relationship, our destiny with Dog was inexorably forged. This is when people most likely first began raising dogs to exhibit certain desirable traits and behaviors conducive to herding, hunting, and guarding.

Bark Like an Egyptian

Examples of our bond with the dog can be found throughout ancient history. Images of dogs abounded in ancient Egypt. In the Cairo museum is displayed a golden knife sheath decorated with canines that dates back to 6,000 B.C. The dog was even elevated to a deity in the form of Anubis, the

Egyptian god of the dead. Whether Anubis was a jackal, a wolf, or a dog, he was undeniably canine. Beloved dogs were even mummified to accompany their masters in the afterlife. The first distinctive breed of dog was the saluki, which originated in dry grasslands of Asia and whose likeness is found in the hieroglyphs of Egyptian tombs. The barkless basenji also harks back to Egyptian times.

Dogs of War and Mythical Mutts

Cave drawings from the Bronze Age in France depict a hunter with a pack of dogs. In ancient civilizations man originally used dogs in hunting and war, but over time their relationship deepened and gradually dogs became more than just hunters and warriors. Somewhere along the way, love entered the picture. Living alongside these helpful creatures that showed no fear or aggression toward humans soon had us looking after the animals and showing them affection, which of course was returned tenfold.

Although still employed mainly for hunting, guarding, and battle, dogs were valued for more than just those qualities by the Greeks and Romans. The dog figures largely in Greek mythology in the third century B.C. In Homer's story, Odysseus had a dog, Argos, who after twenty years of misery and separation from his master, died overjoyed at the warrior's return to Ithaca. Only Odysseus' faithful dog recognized him after such a long absence.

In ancient Rome, Pliny the Elder (43 B.C.–16 A.D.) exalted the dog's psychic qualities and sang the praises of canine fidelity. It wasn't until Roman times that dogs were really developed into defined types such as guard dogs, sporting dogs, shepherds, scent hounds, and sight hounds. And only within the last few hundred years have more specific breeds emerged from the original doggie DNA. Today, there are nearly 400 domestic dog breeds recognized worldwide, and they are as varied in appearance as in function.

It is hard to imagine that every dog breed that exists today, from Newfoundland and Neapolitan to papillon and Pekingese, descended from that prehistoric canid lurking outside Og's cave in hope of a handout. Modern man has had more than a little to do with creating designer doggie genes, and new breeds are still being developed from mixing and mutating the same selection of DNA strands.

Of course, as is the case with most designers, there is sometimes a tendency to get carried away with style trends. This often has some rather bizarre and impractical results, in duds or dogs. Consider the Chinese crested and the shar pei, for example. Yes, I know. Beauty is in the eye of the beholder, and thanks to aging baby boomers, sparse hair and wrinkles are in, even for their dogs. These breeds and other canine oddities certainly bear no resemblance to the feral dogs you still see roaming the streets of villages in some countries, which are similar to what early dogs probably looked like.

Dogs on the Dole

When you observe most domestic dogs these days, at least the ones not earning their kibble in K9-to-5 jobs as helper dogs, guard dogs, or search-and-rescue dogs, you realize it's possible that we may have been too effective in integrating this canine into our society. There has been a price paid for our domesticating the heck out of this formerly wild species.

From Og's dog on down, canines have become dependent on human beings for their very existence. Dogs aren't wolves, and they don't behave exactly as wolves do. They have lost the kill-and-devour instinct of their wolf predecessors, along with many of their other survival instincts—fortunate for us, but sometimes not so lucky for the dog. Stray dogs may form packs and kill livestock, but they don't eat it. They are more engaged in the sport of chasing down the animal than in the killer instinct. It's more play than work, which is certainly no consolation to the victims of the chase or the farmers and ranchers who raise the livestock.

Today's coddled canine has advanced far beyond foraging in the garbage for scraps of meat (unless, of course, it's foraging in the garbage pail for the leftovers from last night's supper). Dogs not only depend on us to bring home the dog chow but also to serve it up on demand, with a hearty helping of chopped beef or chicken and gravy on top, if you please.

No longer must dogs be content to remain on the outside of the family circle looking in. Most often, they're right at the center of our lives, top dogs of the pack, enjoying the love and attention we lavish upon them. Of course, we get something back in return for all that attention; otherwise, we wouldn't be so inclined to do all we do for them. We're self-centered that way. Only the dog practices unconditional love. It's when you're not around to offer him the expected handouts and shower him with attention that his safe little world begins to fall apart.

Social welfare programs are all pretty much the same, whether for people or dogs. A dog on the dole is every bit as dependent as a human being is when he must rely on someone else for his needs. You know the saying: Give a man a fish and you'll feed him for a day; teach him to fish, and you'll feed him for life. It's a little more complicated for the family dog. Even if you could teach him to fish, you'd still have to feed him for life and attend to his other needs. Too bad Uncle Sam doesn't offer tax deductions for dog owners.

No Dog Left Behind

So, you have a stay-at-home dog with no job prospects and too much time on his paws. That can spell trouble if you don't find something worthwhile to occupy his time. A little homeschooling may be in order while you're at work. Since Spot can't clean the house, cook, or surf the Net, he needs something that will engage his doggie senses and invoke the dim remnants of his primeval wolf instincts.

If you've ever watched kids at play, you'll notice that they are usually drawn to activities they're naturally good at. A child's natural abilities are evident at an early age. Some children like to build things with blocks or do physical activities. Some like puzzles and games that challenge their problem-solving skills. Others are more interested in music, art, or reading books. This observation can be applied to engaging your dog in activities. His breed determines his aptitudes, and that will help you choose activities to keep him challenged and happy.

Diary of a Mad Housedog

If your dog kept a diary, any given day might read something like this:

6:00 A.M. I can hear the covers rustling in the bedroom. Well, it's about time she got her lazy bones out of the bed and took me for a walk. Up and at 'em, Missy! I'll go retrieve the leash and be waiting for her when she comes out of the bathroom.

6:25 A.M. Sheesh! Is she ever coming out of there? I have some important pee-mail to check.

6:26 A.M. Finally! Come on, Mom. I'm still waiting for my walk. Let's go!

6:30 A.M. What's this? She went right past me. She's heading for the kitchen in an awful hurry. Guess I'll have to be more a little more persistent.

6:35 A.M. Well, at least I'll get a little something to eat before my walk. She can never resist giving me a handout when I turn on my canine charm.

6:40 A.M. Mmm. That toasted half of a bagel was yummy. Okay, now I'm ready for my walk. Here's the leash. Let's go, already!

6:45 A.M. Hooray, I'm getting somewhere now. She's searching for her keys. Hold on just a doggone minute. Those are the car keys. Hey, maybe she's taking me to the park again. Yippee! I love to go to the park. All those plants to water, squirrels to chase, dog butts to sniff.

7:00 A.M. I can't believe it. She left without me. Just tossed me a couple of biscuits, patted me on the head, and out the door she went. Is she ever coming back? Whatever shall I do?

7:05 A.M. Where is she? She's been gone so long.

7:20 A.M. Where the heck is she? What does she expect me to do with myself here all day long? She must know how I hate to be alone like this with no one to keep me company. I miss her. She didn't even leave me anything to play with.

7:25 A.M. Well, that's it. I'm certain she's never coming back. I've been abandoned. I'm all on my own, left to fend for myself. Arroooooooo! I'll have to find a way out of here and go find her, or I'll go as mad as Old Yeller.

7:30 A.M. But first maybe I'll check out the kitchen and see if I can find some more bagels.

7:45 A.M. Well, I'm glad she forgot to empty the garbage after dinner last night. I had a lot of fun rummaging through it. I managed to lick up most of the gravy drippings off the floor. Oops, I think that load of stuff I just wolfed down is coming back up the chute. I'd better hurry to find a nice clean spot on the Oriental rug to deposit it. I might want seconds later. And the beige suede sofa is always good for wiping my whiskers afterwards. While I'm at it, I might as well bury that greasy beef bone under the cushion to save for a rainy day.

Later the same day . . .

4:00 P.M. Well, my great escape failed. I tried clawing my way through the screen door and the window shade, but I'm trapped like a rat. I'm a prisoner in solitary confinement.

4:30 P.M. Thank doG for pillow therapy. I really chewed the stuffing out of those. Hey, it looks like it's snowing in here!

4:35 P.M. Whew, I'm as dizzy as Toto in a tornado! I keep trying, but I can never catch my tail.

4:45 P.M. Ah, I feel much better after taking my frustrations out on those designer shoes of hers. That Italian leather makes a primo rawhide chewy.

5:00 P.M. Hey, I hear something outside. It's a familiar sound. It's her car coming up the driveway. She's home! She's home! I can't wait to see her. I'll have to show her how happy I am she's finally returned. I'll jump up and down and claw at her legs and lick her face. She'll love that! I just know she'll be as thrilled to see me, too, especially after she sees how I was able to entertain myself so well all day long without her.

5:03 P.M. Oh, boy! That's the sound of the car door slamming. She's almost here! I can hardly wait to see her again. I bet she'll lavish me with love and tell me over and over again what a good dog I am. Then she'll give me an extra special yummy treat, even better than the gravy, the pillows, and the imported Italian chew toy. Best of all, I'll bet she also takes me for that walk I've been waiting for all day long.

Fact is, Fido isn't likely to be greeted with a happy face once his owner sees the wanton destruction that has gone on in her absence. She'll be angry and will blame the dog for all the damage. And wait until she sees her ruined shoes! She may even punish him, but it's not the dog's fault the house is in shambles. He has no clue he's done anything wrong. He's just being himself. What else would you expect a dog to do for ten hours at a stretch—interminable, to his dog brain—but find creative ways to pass the time? He might be a good watchdog, but he doesn't wear a watch, and even if he did, he can't tell what time it is, other than the fact that it's getting dark outside, he wants his walk, and you still aren't home. Until you return, his pack is incomplete, and that's all he knows or cares about.

Your furry little home-wrecker doesn't know that he's done anything that would displease you because that's the very last thing he'd ever want to do. The dog lives to please his master, but he will continue to wreak havoc on the home front until his owner finds ways to keep her dog constructively occupied in her absence. If not, she can expect to continue to encounter a war zone every evening upon returning home—and this was only Monday!

Meeting Your Breed's Needs

When it comes to figuring out how to keep your dog happily engaged in something constructive while you're gone, a good place to start is considering the need for the breed of dog, or if he's not a purebred, then the most predominant breed in the muttly mix. The rules of engagement are as varied as the breeds themselves, but the AKC has made it a little easier for us by grouping the many breeds according to their type and function. Yes, thanks to humans, Dogdom is not a classless society. Your dog falls somewhere within the following groups:

- Sporting Group
- Hound Group
- Working Group
- Terrier Group
- Toy Group
- Nonsporting Group
- Herding Group
- Miscellaneous Class

The dogs within each of these groups share some common physical and behavioral characteristics. Even from the name, it's pretty easy to determine what kinds of activities might be more suitable for a breed in that group. Of course, there are exceptions to every rule. Whether due to nature or nurture, all dogs are individuals.

A Dog for All Seasons

Pointers like to point, even though it's not very polite, and retrievers will retrieve anything retrievable, although the cat isn't always very cooperative. Both are field-and-stream kinds of dogs with a strong hunting heritage. Look at any nineteenth-century painting, and you'll see pastoral scenes depicted of the hunter tooting his own horn with these dogs at his side, most often frozen in a point ready to flush out a pheasant. Dogs do the work; people take the credit. So what else is new?

Dogs in the Sporting Group have tremendous powers of concentration, so you'll want to leave your hunter with something that will keep her focused. If you don't have your own aviary, then a window where your dog can watch wild birds or other animals will help. If he can see a birdhouse or squirrel feeder, all the better. Of course, sometimes they can be a little too focused, so you may have to introduce a post-hypnotic suggestion: When I snap my fingers you will release the cat. Release the cat!

Hounds are hunters, too, but not in the same way as the sporting breeds. Some, such as greyhounds, Afghan hounds, and salukis, are sight hounds that rely on their visual acuity to track game. They are attracted, more than most dogs are, to objects that travel on a horizontal trajectory. Others, such as bloodhounds and basset hounds, are the nose-to-the-grindstone group and were bred to track game by scent.

If you don't happen to have a racing track and rabbit lure to keep your sight hound's interest, you'll need to find an activity that will catch his eye. A Roomba robotic vacuum can serve as a lure for your sight hound, especially if you attach a toy rabbit to the top of it. Scent hounds are easy to please. Just give them something good to sniff out around the house. One way to keep these fellows happy is to hide treats in various places for them to find. They are slow and methodical in their pursuits, so this could keep them busy for quite a while. Be warned that you might have a different interpretation of what's considered good for sniffing—in other words, be sure to empty the garbage and the diaper pail.

Work, work, work. If you own a working breed, you may wonder, "Don't these guys ever take a biscuit break?" The answer is no. They were bred to serve and protect, and that's their prime directive as dogs on the job. These are also generally the larger of the dog breeds. If you have a bored, destructive mastiff or rottweiler on your hands, you have a big problem. All the more reason to find some meaningful work (or at least something that seems like work) for this dog to do, because unlike other employees he'll never whine that he doesn't get enough time off for a vacation. Give your workaholic breed something to guard or protect for maximum job satisfaction. If you have a gentle rottie like Carl of the well-known children's books, you could have a *real* dog sitter. And you can even pay him in dog biscuits.

In Latin, the word *terra* means earth, and terriers really dig it. That's because they were bred to root in the earth for prey such as rabbits, rats, or other small vermin. When a terrier is outdoors, all you are likely to spy of him is his hind end because the other end will be busily excavating a hole in the ground. If you have a terrier in the house, you'll never need to call in an exterminator for rodents. He'll take care of that for you at no charge. Assuming you don't have any mice running around your house, you'll need to find something to keep your hyperactive terrier from becoming a tearier. Provide these dogs with plenty of toys to interact with, chase, or chew to help them expend some of that excess energy.

Toys might be mostly lap dogs that people love to spoil, but they are still dogs. Well, sort of. Many of these, like toy poodles, pinschers, and schnauzers, are just miniaturized versions of standard breeds and have characteristics similar to their larger cousins. Even a toy dog likes to feel useful and have something to do with all that leisure time on his paws. They may be more tolerant of being left indoors for longer periods of time because they were bred to be mostly indoor dogs and are more delicate, but you'll still want to provide your "toy" with some interesting toys to chew on or play with.

Have you heard? Herding breeds love to herd, as anyone who has owned a Border collie or some other kinds of herding breeds can tell you. They'll often nip at your heels as though you and the members of your family were a herd of sheep. In fact, you may often find yourselves collected in the same room of the house with your dog guarding the doorway, staring intently at any stragglers so as not to let any of the herd escape. This is no apartment dweller's dog, and if you don't have a ranch with a few acres and sheep for these breeds to corral, you'll need to be creative in finding ways to help him burn off all that energy—and don't be sheepish about it. Many owners of these active breeds participate frequently in sheepherding trials, which is a sure way to have a little peace when your home isn't on the range.

There are many other breeds, and each has its own needs to fend off ennui. By studying the history and behavioral characteristics of your individual breed of dog—and again, the best time to do this is before you bring a dog into your home—you'll know better how to keep your dog contented in your absence and prevent him from having to endure another dog day afternoon.

Chapter 3

NEVER CAN SAY GOODBYE

In *Romeo and Juliet,* Shakespeare wrote of the sweet sorrow of being apart from the one you love. From your dog's perspective, however, there's nothing sweet about the sorrow of being apart from you. For her, being separated from the object of her affection is a tragedy even the bard never wrote about.

Guilt to Go

I'll bet you thought that your mother was the only one who knew how to dish out a heaping helping of guilt. Ha! Any devoted dog lover knows that when it's time to leave your canine companion behind for any length of time, you can order up some guilt to go, and he'll gladly super-size it for you. No matter how cleverly you think you are concealing your intention to make a clean escape without a scene, your dog always seems to instinctively know when something's afoot and you're about to set a foot out the front door. What tips him off?

You do! It may be the subtlest gesture you might make, some minor variation in your usual routine, or the faintest jingle of car keys (and you tried so hard to be quiet). Even your choice of attire provides him with a vital clue. While not exactly a canine couturier, your Hugo Boss Dog can easily differentiate between your drool-spattered dog-walking duds and your designer business suit. He notices when you are searching for your cell phone, putting things in your briefcase, or stowing the laptop in its carrier for transport. If the suitcase should come out of the closet, you may as well have marched an elephant through the room, because he knows what it means when you start packing your trunk. You are going on safari, and it's likely to be for more than a day.

My Daisy always knew when I was hitting the book promotion trail again when I rolled my wheeled case out of the closet. I also had to be careful about zippers because she associated the zipping sound with my imminent departure. As carefully as I tried to zip them up quietly, her sensitive hearing made her hard to fool. Then she got that look that can make you feel guiltier than your mother ever could. Believe me, no one can look as downcast as a basset hound, even when they aren't actually depressed.

We humans are creatures of habit. No matter how well you may try to disguise your intent, you are signaling your plan of escape to your dog as plainly as if you'd put it on canine cue cards. Your little ham of an actor stages Act One of a heart-rending performance unequaled in Shakespearean tragedies. He gives you that pitiful, pining look and may even shiver and shake a little for added effect. If all else fails, he flings himself onto, or into, your suitcase in the hope of preventing you from packing for that trip. Who among us dog lovers cannot falter when confronted with such high doggie drama? To be gone or not to be gone? That is the question. Face it, we're putty in their paws.

> Some of my most poignant memories are of having to leave my beloved dog Dolly alone all day long while I worked outside the home. She was a rescue dog, and I felt as though I was abandoning her all over again. The last thing I saw every morning as I drove away was Dolly, peering sadly at me through the slats of the fence. She was certainly no sadder than I was at being parted from her best friend for eight long hours every day. I'd cry all the way to work. All I wanted to do was turn around and go back home. Sometimes I did!

> There were no "bring your dog to work" days at my workplace. I occasionally played hooky just to stay at home and keep my dogs company. For the first time, I understood how my mother must have felt when she had to leave her children with babysitters to go off to work each day. In fact, I so disliked leaving my fur children behind that I eventually quit my nine-to-five job and started a home-based business. As it happened, it was my special love for Dolly that encouraged me to make the needed changes in my life that ultimately led me on a more fulfilling career path as a writer. I've never regretted my decision to leave that dead-end job, and I'd do it all over again for the love of a good dog.

Admittedly, most people won't go to such lengths to avoid leaving their dogs home alone. Luckily, there are many other options available to dog owners who want to avoid having a latchkey dog.

Who Let the Dogs In?

Over time, dogs have graduated from being outside most of the time, where they had to fend for themselves in the elements, to staying indoors with their owners, on the sofa or bed. They are living the good life with their humans and loving it. That can make it all the harder for us to leave them on their own for a while.

Even though there are more Fido-friendly places to travel, it's not always possible to take your dog along with you when you take a trip. That means you must make other arrangements for the care of your dog while you are away. There are a greater variety of options available than there used to be, but many people still choose to have a neighbor look in on their dog and feed or walk it in their absence. Too often this ends in disaster, as it did for my neighbors when they returned from vacation. Someone had left the gate open, and their dog was gone. Their distress was not a happy ending to their holiday. My neighbors eventually found their little corgi, but too often the dog is not recovered right away. With every day that passes, the odds for locating a lost pet decrease.

Unfortunately, even when other people offer to watch your dog while you're away, they may not attach as much importance as you would to such things as unlocked gates or doors left ajar. They may not be dog owners themselves, in which case they probably don't understand the precautions necessary to ensure a dog's safety. It's a better idea to take advantage of a more reliable option, one that will assure you of the safety of your pet while you're away from home.

Critter Sitters

Daycare isn't just for toddlers anymore. Doggie daycare is the preferred choice of more and more working people who want to make certain that their dog is well cared for while they are at the office. The trained staff at these facilities keep the dogs happy and entertained and also provide training for their four-legged charges. A standing rule at doggie daycare is that dogs must be fully inoculated and well socialized with other dogs. Some facilities even have special training sessions if your dog has some behavior issues or fitness programs if your hound is too round. Visit a doggie daycare, and you'll be hard pressed to find a dog that does not look like he's having a wonderful time. Just don't forget to bring your earplugs. With a dozen or so dogs all barking in chorus, it can get pretty noisy at times.

Mary Puppins

Perhaps your dog isn't quite as social as some are or is old and infirm and might not do as well in daycare, which can be a bit boisterous at times. Some dogs are happier on their own turf in their owner's absence, and it is less upsetting for them than being taken to a strange place. Many dogs do not fare well when left in kennels, barking incessantly or refusing to eat because they are pining for their owners.

Maybe you just prefer to have individualized, at-home care of your pet while you're away. If so, you can always hire a nanny. The perfect nanny must have a kind heart and be ready to shower your dog with tender loving care—the same qualities you'd expect of someone taking care of your child.

Professional dog sitters are first and foremost devoted dog lovers, and very often dog trainers, who are well accustomed to handling dogs. Many have worked in some other form of animal-related profession before launching their own pet-sitting businesses. One woman left her lucrative veterinary practice to become a professional dog sitter. She said that the reason she changed careers was because she found her adventures in pet sitting more joyful and fulfilling than her interaction with ailing and dying pets in a clinical setting. Her former experience as a trained veterinarian was no doubt an added bonus to her clients.

A sitter will come and look in on your dog, play with him, exercise him, and feed and water him. Your dog nanny will also administer medications, although it may be a spoonful of peanut butter or cream cheese instead of sugar that helps the medicine go down.

Five-Bone Hotels

If you simply can't bear to leave your dog behind while you travel, you'll be happy to know that more hotels are rolling out the red carpet for Rover. Checking in with a four-legged guest has become the rule rather than the exception for travelers. Room service in some five-bone hotels offers Omaha steaks and carob treats on Fido's pillow; of course, that would be the pillow next to yours if your dog sleeps with you.

Hotels such as the new Wag Hotel that recently opened in Sacramento, California, the first in a chain of premier doggie hotels to be built across the United States, are putting their best paw forward to accommodate the lap dogs of luxury in a style that they and their owners have come to expect. Wag Hotels have expanded the concept of boarding your dog way beyond the traditional lockdown. Instead, they offer a home away from home for your beloved pet, including fenced play yards, carefully selected playmates, activities, massage, "people furniture," plasma TVs, artwork, and even a swimming pool. Most people hotels I've stayed in aren't that swanky. Wag Hotels even offer Happy Tail Ale, a nonalcoholic beer for dogs, to their canine guests. Let the Yappy Hour begin!

Chateau du Chien

Being in the doghouse doesn't mean quite the same thing that it once did. Not so long ago, most dogs lived strictly outdoors, and the doghouse consisted of a drafty lean-to, often with no insulation against the harsh elements. That has changed, though, and so have doghouses. As we've become more concerned about the comfort and well-being of our companion animals, doghouses have improved quite a lot. Some are even miniatures of Victorian and Georgian mansions or other barketectural marvels. The Dogloo, which looks like an Eskimo igloo, provides much better insulation than did the little doghouse on the prairie. These days, the doghouse is likely to have all the comforts of home. That's because the dog's house probably *is* your home!

Furry Feng Shui

Perhaps your abode could use a little furry feng shui to make it even more habitable for Fido. In case you aren't already familiar with the concept of feng shui, the objective is to create a living space that allows the unobstructed flow of energy, or ch'i. Ch'i (pronounced chee) is the life force or "breath" that flows through all living things. In this case, of course, we're talking dog breath.

"Feng shui" literally means "wind and water." The concept underlying feng shui is that living spaces should delight the inhabitant and promote harmony, health, and a feeling of well-being. It's just as important for our dogs to be at ease in their living spaces as it is for us. How comfortable is your dog's environment? Does he have his own space in the home? If you're like some people I know, your dog has a room of his own, complete with TV and a toy box that's regularly replenished with new playthings so the dog doesn't get bored. Making your dog's home turf comfortable and appealing to his senses can only enhance his quality of life. By creating a harmonious balance of yang (bright, open spaces) and yin (quiet, dark spaces), not only will you benefit from a more serene scene, you'll also unblock the flow of ch'i in your Chihuahua.

Another important thing in feng shui is water, which carries ch'i. With that in mind, you may want to consider relocating the dog's water bowl. If the water bowl is in an area of heavy foot traffic, that could be detrimental to the flow of the dog's ch'i, although it's never detrimental to the flow of water spilling all over your kitchen floor when you accidentally kick the bowl over. If his water bowl of choice is the toilet, you won't be able to relocate his water source without a home renovation, but at least you'll know the directional flow of the water and where it exits, which are also important feng shui considerations.

Fido-friendly feng shui would provide your dog with an area facing south or southeast to catch the early morning warmth of the sun's rising. No feng shui master designed my house, but fortunately it has a southern exposure. First thing every morning, I open the front door and window blinds to create a sunny spot for my "sundogs" to bask in, which they relish. By the same token, they seek out quieter spots in the house in the afternoon for their naptime. Dogs will often seek a quiet space in the house if there's noise that interferes with their beauty sleep; this is particularly true of basset hounds, which despite their appearance seem to require an inordinate amount of beauty sleep. Dogs also do this when they are ailing. If you notice that your dog is suddenly sleeping in different places than usual, get him to the veterinarian for a thorough exam. He could have a health problem you're not aware of.

It's important to provide good ventilation and circulation of fresh air in your home. Feng shui dictates that houses be designed to allow a natural flow of air through the house. Areas where the air gets stagnant are not considered beneficial to health or well-being. If you live in a house that tends to get stuffy, open the windows now and then. That way your dog won't have to spend so much time hanging his head out the car window to get a little fresh air.

You should also arrange furniture that allows convenient access to all parts of the house. At least clear the path to the dog door. If your dog has vision problems, this could be especially important.

Bubba's Night Light

Shortly after we adopted our basset hound Bubba Gump, I heard him whining in the middle of the night. At first, when I couldn't find him anywhere, I thought something must be terribly wrong. I followed the pitiful cries and finally found him out in the dark garage, frozen in place in the narrow avenue leading from the outer dog door to the one in the kitchen door. It was then I realized that he was afraid of the dark! After my husband cleared a better path and installed a nightlight in the garage for Bubba, we never had any further problems with our scaredy dog.

Whether it's for human inhabitants or their fur friends, feng shui is concerned with creating health and happiness and improving life in the here and now. Of course, our comparatively short-lived dogs have always had an innate understanding of how important is it to be happy in the present; they didn't need feng shui to figure that out.

In the Beanie and Cruiser Mystery Series, my sleuth, Elsie MacBean (Beanie) often takes cues from her canine sidekick, Cruiser, by observing how he reacts to people. If the normally friendly Cruiser doesn't respond positively to someone Beanie meets, she knows there must be a very good reason. In all my mystery novels, Cruiser is instrumental in helping Beanie solve the crimes because of his intuitive nature and, of course, that keen nose of his.

I'm the same way with my own dogs as Beanie is with Cruiser. I always notice my dog's reaction to people because I've found that there's no better judge of human character than a dog. Knowing the gregarious nature of the basset hound, I am wary of someone if my dog reacts to him or her in a negative way. Of course, there are some exceptions to the rule. If Bubba takes an instant dislike to someone after an introductory sniff, it could simply be that he's concluded she's a cat lover. Bubba hates cats!

Honest to doG

No matter whether you're talking to people or to dogs, honesty is the best policy. In fact, dogs can see through guile more quickly than most humans can. They understand more than you think they do. Don't tell your dog you're just going to the market if the market is in France—unless you live in France, of course. Sacre bleu!

Dogs are much more fluent in people talk than we are in dog speak. While we may think we need a Bow-Lingual translator to understand our dogs, they need no such techie device to understand our language perfectly. Dogs can understand as many as 200 words in their owner's vocabulary and can read human physical and emotional cues better than most people. It often seems that they can predict our actions and sense the motives behind them even before the synapses have connected in our own brains. Perhaps it's their sensitivity to our needs that makes them so indispensable and so doggone hard for us to leave for very long.

Parting Is Such Sweet Sorrow

Shakespeare wasn't writing about Juliet's lapdog, but as far as most dog lovers are concerned, Juliet could just as well have been soliloquizing about her distress at being parted from the Capulet family pooch. In fact, books and films are full of stories about the pain of being parted from our dogs, whether it's for a night, a fortnight, or longer. What greater tragedy is there than unrequited love, whether between young lovers or young dog lovers?

When former Beatle John Lennon wrote his famous lyrics about the need for love, he could have been writing about the lost dog of his childhood. His uncle gave him an adorable puppy, but his cat-loving aunt Mimi gave the puppy away. John's heart was broken. Is it any wonder he often seemed so cynical as an adult? Who can say what psychological damage it does to be separated so young from something you love so much, and who knows how long the emotional scar would linger? Parents often underestimate the strength and importance of that early bond with a pet and how quickly that bond can form. I'm grateful my parents never gave any of my dogs away. If what John sang about needing love is true, then all you need is a dog.

Nothing is guaranteed to elicit tears of emotion more than the "boy loves dog, boy loses dog, boy finds dog" formula in fiction or film. What's worse is when the dog doesn't come back. There should be a special award in Hollywood just for these tail-wagging tearjerkers. Here are a few of the classics:

Lassie Come Home—This tale glorifies the loyalty of dogs at all costs when a penniless British family sells their beloved collie in order to make ends meet. But Lassie escapes a cruel master and makes a hazardous journey back home to return to her boy.

The Pooch—In this Little Rascals film, Stymie and the Gang manage to rescue Petie from the dogcatcher, and not a moment too soon. If Matthew "Stymie" Beard, Jr., didn't receive an award for his tearful performance, he certainly should have. Petie the Pooch didn't do so bad, either.

The Incredible Journey—Two dogs and a cat cross the Canadian wilderness and suffer great hardships to be reunited with their family.

Where the Red Fern Grows—This film about the life adventures of two redbone hounds and the boy who raises them, loves them, and ultimately buries them where the red fern grows gets a ten-tissue rating. Better make that a whole box of tissues.

Goodbye, My Lady—A boy, Jesse, finds a basenji lost in the Louisiana bayou and proves his maturity to his grandfather when he must ultimately surrender his beloved Lady to her rightful owner, never to see her again. Even the dog cries in this one.

The Call of the Wild—You'll want to snuggle up with a St. Bernard like Buck when you watch the film adaptation of Jack London's classic tale of the Alaskan Klondike. Buck and his owner encounter danger and adventure in the frozen north, and Buck's master must ultimately release his beloved companion when he answers the call of nature and we learn what a dog does in the woods; that is, Buck becomes leader of the wolf pack.

Old Yeller—After all these years, I still can't talk about this one without choking up. Shoot! I'm not the only person who bears emotional scars from that doggone story. Impressionable children should not be subjected to this film without a psychologist to talk them through it. You'll save them years of costly therapy later on.

Happy Homecoming

When you were a kid, you may remember the anticipation you felt while waiting for your mom or dad to come home from work every evening. Minutes passed like hours as you waited to hear the welcome sound of the car pulling into the driveway and the slam of the car door. You listened intently for your father's whistle as he walked to the front door. Perhaps he might even have brought you a special treat hidden in his coat pocket or in his lunch pail, as my dad used to do. Then the door opened and the moment you'd been waiting for arrived. You'd run to greet him, leap up into his arms, and kiss his face.

Fur kids are no different. If you don't have children, then your dog is probably the only one in your household that will ever greet you with that much enthusiasm. (That may be the case even if you do have kids.) Is it any wonder we love dogs so? Who wouldn't love being greeted like a rock star every time he walked through the front door? It doesn't matter if you've been gone for five minutes or five weeks, the response never wavers. In fact, sometimes you wonder if you shouldn't leave more often, just so you can bask in all the adulation upon your return.

Often we're so harried in our everyday lives that we forget to adequately return all the adoration that our dogs give us so freely, but we are only human after all. When we come in the door, we're tired and distracted, already thinking about what to defrost for dinner or checking phone messages or e-mail. Maybe we give the dog a perfunctory pat on the head on the way to the kitchen.

Next time you come home from work, forget about all the household stuff for a little while and take time to really greet your dog the way she deserves. Come down to her level and caress her. Let her search for that treat in your coat pocket you stashed for her to find or invite her to explore your lunch pail for leftovers. Maybe you even bought her a new toy on the way home. Tell her what a good dog she is, and take her out for a walk. Play with her for a while.

You'll be surprised how beneficial this will be, not only for your dog but also for you. After all, it's been a long day for both of you. Take time to relax and spend some quality time with your best friend. Isn't that why you got a dog in the first place? You can always clean up the breakfast dishes and defrost the chops later. That's why they invented dishwashers and microwaves, so you and your dog can enjoy a happy homecoming.

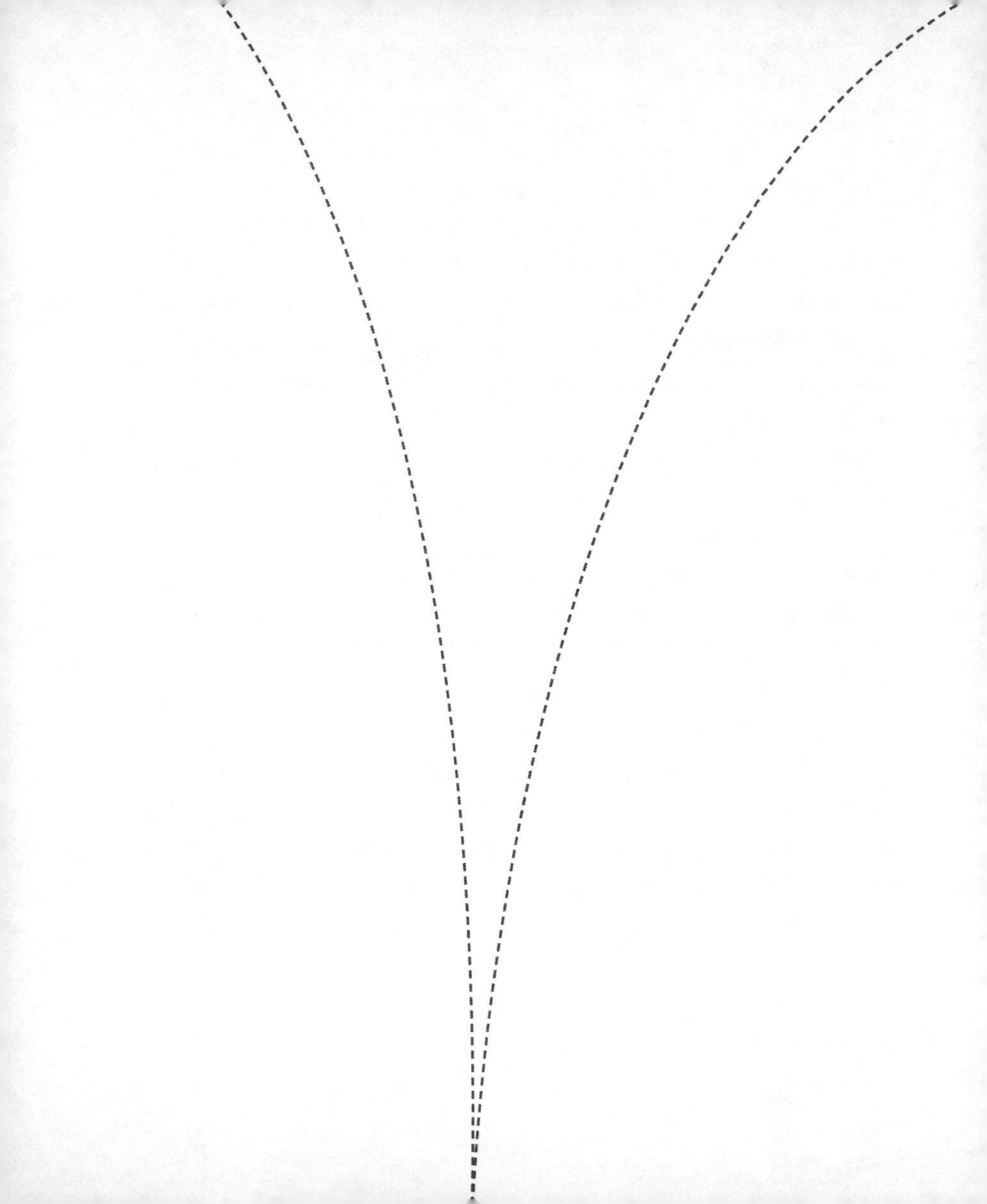

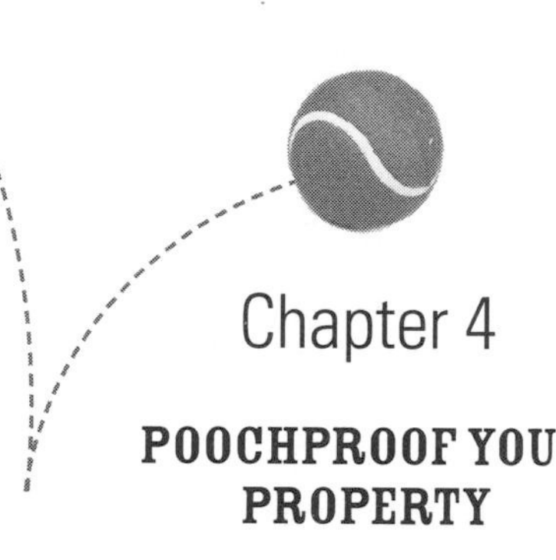

Chapter 4

POOCHPROOF YOUR PROPERTY

Parents of small children know all about the importance of babyproofing to make sure that children stay out of mischief while Mommy's back is turned. When they are busy or away from home, responsible dog parents should be every bit as concerned for the safety of their fur children. Taking a few minutes before you leave to spot-check your house for pet safety can save you some expense and trouble and could even save your pet's life.

Although your child isn't as likely to chew up your Prada pumps, pups can get into just as much mischief as kids do. As is the case with toddlers, everything finds its way into a puppy's mouth, and I still have the vacuum cleaner with the duct-taped electrical cord to prove it. Fortunately, the Hoover wasn't plugged in when our little basset Bramble decided the cord would make a fine chew toy. A garden hose met the same fate with another of our puppies, Butterscotch.

I'll bet she was surprised when that long green snake sprung a leak and gave her a shot of water up the snout.

Back to Basics

Before you leave the house, the most important thing is to be sure that your dog's basic needs have been provided for. Leaving him supplied with all the toys and chewies in the world won't matter if you've forgotten to supply him with what he needs for survival. We're not talking about Y2K-9 hoarding, just a few necessities for your best friend's safety and comfort.

Animal Shelter

Many people assume that because dogs have a fur coat, they are impervious to the weather. While dogs with thicker coats, such as huskies and malamutes, do fare better in cold climates, shorter-haired dogs don't have as much natural protection when the mercury dips in the winter. This is probably why they allow you to dress them in silly-looking sweaters and booties, though they may hope their four-legged homies don't see them that way.

Whether short- or long-coated, every dog deserves a shelter of some kind. If your dog does not stay in the house (and I sincerely hope he does because he should be considered part of your family), then you must provide him with a warm, dry habitat to protect him from the elements. His doghouse doesn't need to have central heat and air—although that would certainly be nice—but it should be well insulated and devoid of drafts. As discussed in the previous chapter, doghouses have been much improved over the years and are now much better designed to protect dogs against the cold and heat.

Made in the Shade

One thing people often fail to consider in warmer weather is whether their dog has ample shade from the sun's rays. A canine wearing a sun visor and dog goggles might look pretty cool, but it takes more than that to keep him cool. Dogs do not sweat in the same way that humans do. They cool themselves mainly by panting. Dogs also perspire through the pads of their feet and the leather of their noses, but it's not a very efficient cooling system in hot weather. Dogs can quickly overheat if left in the sun for very long. Of course, you never should leave your dog in a car in warm weather, or at any other time for that matter. The temperature in a car rises very quickly in the sun and can soar to over 120 degrees. It takes only twenty minutes on a hot summer day for a dog left in a car to suffer heatstroke, which can be deadly. The same fate can and does happen to dogs that are tethered to doghouses or left in dog runs. Even if your dog's house or kennel was in full shade when you left the dog there in the morning, it may be in full sun by afternoon. Make certain that your dog's space is adequately shaded throughout the entire day and that cool water is available. Of course, if your dogs are anything like my spoiled hounds, they are probably lounging around in an air-conditioned house sipping chilled Happy Tail Ale.

Fed and Watered

While feeding and watering may seem pretty bare bones when it comes to dog care, it's still worth mentioning. People can get so harried rushing off to work that they may neglect to fill the dog's dish with kibble or freshen her water in the morning. Fortunately, there are far more reliable feeding and watering systems that can ensure there is always food available and fresh water on tap. Some feeders even allow your dog to dispense his own food. However, if Fido is a foodie, you probably won't want to give him unlimited kibble control or you'll also have to buy him a membership at 24-Hour Fido Fitness.

Leapdog and Tunnel King

Some dogs go over the fence, others go under it, but the end goal is always the same: to escape your yard and gain freedom from boredom. In every neighborhood, there seems to be a leapdog or a tunnel king, and despite every attempt by owners to keep their dogs contained in the yard, nothing seems to work. Most escapees are unneutered male dogs. While neutering is the best deterrent for roaming behavior, there are still those untamed rovers that give Colonel Klink the slip no matter how many nights they spend in the cooler. When it comes to foiling the Great Escape, here are some fence fix-its to employ:

- **Check the entire perimeter of the yard for possible escape routes.** Are any slats missing from the fence? You'd be amazed at what a small space your big dog can squeeze through. The one time our basset escaped from our yard was through a gap in a picket fence no more than five inches wide, which is why we suspect Houdini had to have been reincarnated as a basset hound. These nose slaves are unequaled escape artists.

- **Fix any gaps, loose posts, or sagging gates.** If the next storm huffs and puffs and blows your fence down, your dog will no doubt seize the opportunity to blow the joint, too. Setting fence posts in concrete and laying a concrete base under the fence line will prevent your mutt mole from digging a hole.
- **Sometimes even the tallest fence can't keep a determined dog down.** Some dogs are so good at scaling heights that you'd swear they used a pogo stick to clear the fence. The best way to prevent this is to build a fence that is tilted inward at the top. That will ground even the most skilled leapdog, since he probably hasn't yet figured out how to defy gravity.

Toys and Tidbits

There may not be manufacturer recalls for unsafe dog toys, as there are for children's toys and other people products, but perhaps there should be. Many dog owners have a tale of woe about the toy that got stuck in his dog's throat or about the treat that created an intestinal blockage requiring surgery. Perhaps the offending toy or treat was even fatal to the dog. Such tragedies happen more often than you might imagine when a dog is left unattended with an unsafe toy or chew meant to occupy his time and deter him from chewing up your valuables. The fact is that dogs frequently bite off more than they can chew.

Follow the Bouncing Ball

For instance, hard as it may be to believe, tennis balls can be dangerous toys for dogs. How can that be when they bounce so well and dogs love to chase them so? That's because they are filled with air. If the dog punctures the ball, she can rip it into smaller pieces which, if swallowed, can effectively cork the dog's windpipe, causing her to suffocate if you are not there to extract them in time. If your dog is into retrieving, then leave her with a ball that is designed especially for dogs that love to chase and chew.

No Bones About It

Other objects can splinter, tear, or shred when your dog chews on them, so choose your dog's playthings as carefully as you would those for a toddler. Don't offer cooked beef bones; those can splinter in the dog's intestines or cause impaction and all kinds of problems. Even uncooked bones can be hazardous if they are too small. Poultry bones are definitely out, although some people claim that if they are well cooked to the point of being soft, it's okay.

There are differing opinions on the wisdom of offering bones to dogs. Dr. Billinghurst's Biologically Appropriate Raw Food (BARF) diet touts that bones are an important nutritional element in the pup food pyramid. I do not give my dogs bones of any kind to chew and never will. This is partly because I've had a string of basset hounds with touchy tummies, and I grew tired of cleaning foul globs of partially digested bone off my carpet. But it's also because of an unpleasant childhood memory of when my Brownie troop toured a veterinary surgery, where I saw a cat with a poultry bone sticking out its throat. The pitiful sight of that poor cat made a lasting negative impression on me about giving bones to pets.

Then there was the time one of our bassets got a beef rib bone stuck in the roof of her mouth. Patience was acting very strangely and kept pawing at her snout in a most peculiar manner. At first I thought she was just playing, but then I realized something was wrong. Thinking she might be choking, I probed her throat with my index finger. It was then that I felt the rib bone that had become firmly wedged in the roof of her mouth. It took me a while struggling with a squirming dog, but I finally managed to extract the bone. After that experience, I knew for certain what the rib bone is connected to: trouble for dogs.

Mutts and Chews

Size matters, especially when it comes to dog toys. Match the size of the toy to the dog's breed and age. That is, choose toys that a toy dog breed or puppy can't easily swallow or choke on. The same is true for larger dogs. Don't give them a ball that's too small. A too-small ball is likely to end up stuck in a windpipe.

Even rawhide chews can create problems for dogs. Once the chews get mushy from the dog's saliva, they can also get stuck in places they shouldn't. It's best to take time to evaluate what kinds of chew toys will present no hazard to your dog, but most owners would agree that you can't go wrong with a Kong. You can fill it with an assortment of delectable goodies that will keep your dog busy and engaged without endangering his health or safety. There are also some great interactive treat dispensers available that not only can entertain but also train even the most bored dog.

All That and a Tag and Chips

When it comes to addressing your dog's identity issues, the most important thing is to be sure that he has some form of ID on him at all times that includes your address and phone number. For getting your lost dog home to you quickly, nothing beats the good old dog tag attached to a securely fastened collar. It's worked for decades and is still one of the most reliable ways for reuniting dogs with their owners.

Tag, You're It!

Dog tags have two big things going for them: They're inexpensive and immediately visible. Some even glow in the dark. Of course, dog tags can be lost, and too frequently owners forget to update them when they move or go on vacation. If your dog gets lost while you're vacationing at Disney World, your address and phone number in Kalamazoo, Michigan, won't be much help in getting him returned to you. You won't be home to answer the phone! Some people order special collars with their phone number printed on the fabric, which is more likely to stay on the dog, but the information still has to be current for it to work.

The kind of collar you leave on your dog is also important. Leather or cloth collars are best and should match the measurement of the circumference of the dog's neck. If your dog has outgrown his collar, get him fitted with a new one. Just as you can't still wear your baby shoes, your dog is too big for the collar he wore as a pup. Check for worn or frayed fasteners or holes, and make sure the collar is not too loose or too tight on the dog's neck. You should be able to slip two fingers comfortably under the collar when it's fastened. Never, I repeat, *never* leave a choke chain on your dog when you're away. These collars are for training only when you're at the other end of the leash to use it properly. Choke chains can easily get snagged on fences or other objects with disastrous results. Trust me, this is one hangdog look you never want to see.

Hello, Mr. Chips

Having a chip on your shoulder is a good thing for a dog, especially if it happens to be a microchip. Having a readable microchip embedded in your dog provides extra insurance that he will be returned to you in the event that he is ever lost. In the decade since its inception, pet microchipping has reunited hundreds of thousands of pets with their owners. A Washington dog named Griffey was returned to his owners after six years, thanks to a little microchip.

The microchip is really a tiny computer chip that is programmed with an identification number assigned specifically to your pet. If your pet is ever lost, the registration number on the chip is detected using a special handheld scanner. An identification number appears in a viewing window on the scanner and is matched with the owner's contact information, which is stored in a database. The chip is about the size of a grain of rice, small enough to pass through a special hypodermic needle, and is implanted deeply under the loose skin between the dog's shoulder blades. Some scanners also emit a beep to alert shelter personnel, animal control officers, or veterinarians to the presence of the chip.

You can have the microchip procedure done at a veterinary office, at your local shelter, or at microchipping clinics held in some communities. The cost ranges from $15 to $40, depending on where you have it done, and there's usually an additional registration fee to list the ID in the database, usually no more than $20.

The Illustrated Dog

Your dog doesn't have to wear a leather jacket and ride a Harley Davidson to sport a tattoo. Only this tattoo won't say "Born to Ride" or "Bad to the Bone," and you don't have to take your dog to a tattoo parlor to have it done. A numerical tattoo is a reliable method of dog identification and can be applied by most veterinarians. Although the procedure has been outdated somewhat by the introduction of microchip technology, breeders still routinely use tattoos as proof of identity for their registered dogs. The problem with tattoos is that they are not always easily located or readable. They can fade, and the markings may become distorted or hard to read as your dog grows, but they are still positive proof of ownership.

If you opt for the tattoo, you must register it with an organization such as National Dog Registry, which keeps the number on file and will locate you if someone happens to find your dog and calls in the number. Without registration, which costs around $35, the number is useless, and that tattoo on Bowser's bicep may as well say "Born to Lose."

Lassie, Phone Home!

A collie wanders lost and forlorn on the lonely moors among the heather and ragged gorse. Suddenly, she hears a familiar voice carried across the rolling dales. She pricks up her ears to listen. Lassie! Lassie! Can you hear me now?

Timmy might have found Lassie a lot faster if she'd only had a PetsCell, the first cell phone for dogs. You can forget about photocopiers and staple guns because you won't need to print and post any more lost dog flyers. You can talk to your dog over the two-way speaker attached to his collar, and he can bark right back to you.

The device sells for around $400 and also is equipped with GPS technology that allows you to track your dog's whereabouts. That may seem like a lot of money to spend on such a gadget, but when your best friend goes missing, you'd probably gladly pay much more in reward money for his safe return. PetsCell even has built-in temperature sensors so you know if your dog is too hot or too cold. It can also support a wireless camera that could serve well in search and rescue or bomb squad missions. Doggie daycare patrons may be able to use the device as a canine version of the nanny cam to check up on their dogs. PetsCell also has a "call owner" button, so whoever finds Rover can immediately call you and let you know where he is.

The first fifteen minutes after a dog strays are crucial to its safe return, and PetsCell can help you more quickly pinpoint the exact location of your dog and help ensure that Lassie always comes home. We can only hope that dogs never attend the theater or learn how to drive a car.

Odd Couples

If the members of your household fight like cats and dogs, the reason could be that they are cats and dogs. While some cats and dogs do get along quite well living together—yes, I have witnessed this phenomenon—not all of them do. Cats can also have disagreements with other cats over territorial issues, like who gets to sleep on the top floor of the cat condo. Some dogs don't get along so well with each other, either, particularly if you have two dogs constantly vying to be leader of the pack. Confrontations over choice toys or tidbits can get downright ugly sometimes and can require a referee.

I have heard of many cases in which a new dog or cat has been adopted into a home where one or more dogs already reside. The owner, assuming that they will be fine on their own, returns to the house to find that he was wrong. Some breeds of dog are more aggressive and territorial than others, so in such cases it's especially important to properly introduce a new pet, which may be perceived by your dog as an interloper. Puppies can be particularly vulnerable if thrown in the mix with adult dogs.

No matter how many pets you have, it's vital to ensure that they are well acquainted before you leave them alone together. That doesn't usually happen overnight, so if you know you will have to be away for a while, hire a full-time pet sitter just in case any disagreements arise. Herbal preparations like Rescue Remedy can help pets ease into new homes and can also help other pets accept the newcomer. It's also best not to leave anything with the dogs that could cause disagreements to erupt, like a favorite toy or treats. If you think siblings can be competitive over their stuff, you've never seen two dogs quarrel over a gnarled wedge of rawhide.

K9-1-1

If you have a pet emergency and try dialing K9-1-1 on your telephone, you aren't likely to see an ambulance arrive at your house or a team of paramedics hastening to attend to your pet's health crisis. The closest thing to pet paramedics in our metropolitan area is a mobile veterinary clinic, but there are so few of these, and their services are in such high demand, that the response is hardly ever immediate. They are also not generally equipped to deal with severe trauma. Indeed, there are pet rescue services available in some areas, and the fire department typically performs emergency care and rescue for pets in case of fire or other disasters, but this much-needed pet emergency service is still not as commonplace as it is for humans.

It's vital to ensure that someone can respond to any pet emergency that could arise while you're away. Make certain that someone has your contact information in case of emergency. Also, specify which veterinary clinic people should contact in case your dog becomes ill or is injured while you're away. It's good to have someone available who knows your dog's medical history. If your pet requires medication, you'll need to plan ahead for that, too. It's probably a good idea to let your vet know you'll be out of town and who'll be minding the menagerie.

No Pet Left Behind

What if a natural disaster struck without warning? Who would be responsible for your pet's survival in such emergencies? We often make detailed escape plans for our families in case of an emergency, but what about your pets? They're family, too!

Probably more than any other event in American history, Hurricane Katrina dramatically underscored the necessity of providing care and shelter for pets as well as for people in such a catastrophe.

If there's any silver lining to be found in the devastation caused by Hurricane Katrina, it's that for the first time the status of companion animals was elevated in the consciousness of the American public, government agencies, and the press, all of whom sometimes tend to diminish the significance of pets in people's lives. While at first camera crews were instructed not to film the scenes in New Orleans of animal suffering in deference to that of people, the plight of pets in such severe distress could no longer be ignored. Those unforgettable images must dictate that in future cases of emergency or disaster, our animal companions will never again be an afterthought.

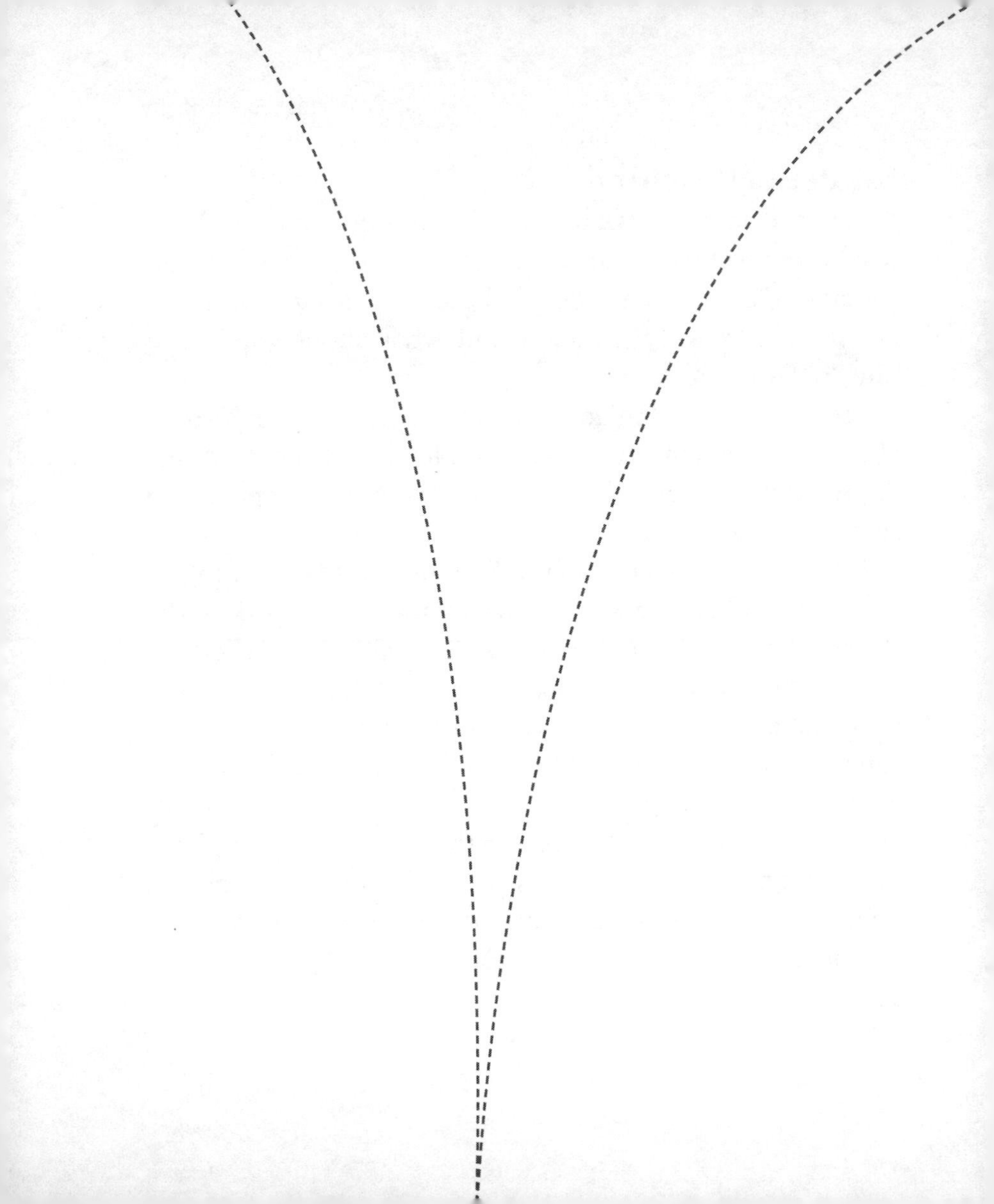

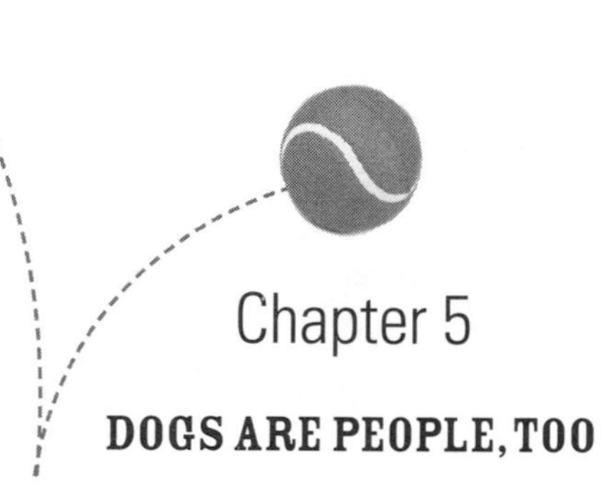

Chapter 5

DOGS ARE PEOPLE, TOO

When I was a kid, I loved Mickey Mouse. I especially loved the fact that he had a dog named Pluto, which was my favorite planet in the solar system because it was the smallest one of the group, like me. Strange as it may seem for a mouse to keep a dog as a pet, Disney's cartoon characters' relationship underscores how important a role a dog can play in one's life, even in the life of a mouse.

Our dogs do a lot for us. They are always there through thick and thin, ever seeking our approval, as Pluto sought Mickey's. We have such high expectations of our dogs, but there are a few things that our dogs should expect from us in return for all that unconditional love and devotion they give us.

Men are from Mars, Dogs are from Pluto

Perhaps the most wonderful thing about dogs is that they are such uncomplicated creatures. They're the best things that ever happened to human beings. They don't need self-help books to understand one another or to know how to have good relationships with people. It's the canine Plutonian's easygoing nature and simplicity that makes him the perfect companion for a human being (or a mouse).

Of Mice and Dogs

Pluto was always eager to make his master happy, but Mickey was sometimes hard to please. What would you expect of a spoiled movie star mouse? He was always putting Pluto through his paces and making him do tricks to impress his mousy girlfriend, Minnie, or that hot-tempered, double-talking duck friend of his, The Donald. It's "Pluto, fetch this! Pluto fetch that! No, Pluto! Down, Pluto!" In short, Mickey treated Pluto like—well, like a dog.

When you consider that a dog is quite a bit higher up on the evolutionary scale than a rodent, Pluto deserves considerable credit for tolerating all this from a mouse. In fact, it's probably a good thing for Mickey that Pluto wasn't a rat terrier. Pluto always knew exactly who he was and was completely secure in his dogness. In fact, he was more interested in flirting with the cute little Pekingese perched on the next bench than in winning some silly old dog show. In the end, Pluto outshone all the fancy purebreds and saved the day by rescuing the object of his affection from a raging fire. Pluto, my hero.

Top 10 Dog Peeves About Humans

1. Dog sweaters. Hello? Haven't you noticed the fur?
2. Yelling at me for barking . . . I'm a freakin' dog!
3. Taking me for a walk, then not letting me check out the grass, the poles, and the smells on the ground. Exactly whose walk is this, anyway?
4. Any trick that involves balancing food on my nose. Just stop it!
5. Any haircut that involves bows or ribbons. Now you know why we chew your stuff up when you're not home.
6. The sleight of hand, fake fetch throw. You fooled a dog! Woohoo, what a proud moment for the top of the food chain.
7. Taking me to the vet for the "big snip," then acting surprised when I freak out afterward.
8. Getting upset when I sniff the crotches of your guests. Sorry, but I haven't quite mastered that handshake thing yet.

9. Blaming your farts on me—not funny, not funny at all!
10. Acting disgusted when I lick myself. Look, we both know the truth: You're just jealous.

Plutonian Properties

If there were a self-help book on relationships titled *Men Are from Mars, Dogs Are from Pluto,* it might list these basic qualities of Plutonians:

- A Plutonian will never try to change you. He likes you just the way you are, even if you don't have four legs and a tail.
- Plutonians are great listeners. That's because they can't talk.
- When Plutonians say they love you, they really mean it, and they say it with actions, which always speak louder than words.
- Plutonians never offer unsolicited advice; in fact, they never offer any advice at all.
- Plutonians are always sensitive to your feelings and are always ready to lend a sympathetic ear, or paw.
- Plutonians love long walks in the park, especially if there are lots of trees.

- Plutonians are intuitive. They always know when it's time to eat or take a walk.
- Plutonians are not only good heelers but also good healers.
- Plutonians will never leave dirty socks or underwear all over the floor, but they might chew them up or hide them from you.
- Plutonians won't leave the toilet seat up, but they might drink from the toilet.
- Plutonians won't channel surf, unless it's time for Animal Planet, of course.
- Plutonians won't complain about how you wash the dishes, but they'll happily lick them clean for you.
- A Plutonian won't criticize your driving, as long as you keep a window rolled down so he can hang his head out.
- Plutonians don't care how late you come home, only that you come home.
- Plutonians don't mind if your shirt doesn't match your pants. In fact, they probably can't even tell.
- Plutonians won't nag you about eating those greasy potato chips on the new furniture. In fact, they'll probably help you eat them and then wipe their whiskers on the sofa.

- Plutonians don't care if you drink out of the milk carton. Look at what they drink out of!
- Plutonians don't expect Martians or Venusians to behave exactly like a Plutonian; otherwise, you'd already be perfect—you'd be a dog.

Bored or Sick?

Does your dog lie around on the sofa all day long? Is she uninterested in things? If you summon her, does she barely respond or even ignore you entirely? If so, then you are probably the owner of a bored dog. However, a lethargic, disinterested dog could also be a sick dog, especially if she shows no interest in eating or playing with you. If your dog is suddenly not her usual buoyant self, or if she is hiding from you or sleeping in different places than usual, you could have a sick dog on your hands.

To maintain your dog's optimum health, it's important to take her to the veterinarian for a yearly checkup and a blood panel workup. Yes, you'll probably spend more than a few dollars on your pet's physical exam by the time all is said and done, but that checkup may save you far greater expense and heartache down the road if diseases are diagnosed and treated early. Those tests may save her life.

Here are some signs of illness to watch for in your dog:

- Change in appetite
- Frequent urination or difficulty in eliminating
- Reduced activity level
- Limping
- Coughing
- Labored or rapid breathing

It's especially important before you leave home on your business trip or vacation to have your dog's health assessed and make sure that she is not ill. In fact, if you board your dog or leave her at doggie daycare, you will be required to provide a certificate of health from your veterinarian stating that your dog is current on all vaccinations, including bordatella, the clinical term for kennel cough.

You know those people who respond to a casual, "How are you doing today?" with an excruciating list of every ache and pain. By the time their stories are done, which could involve foldout diagrams from *Grey's Anatomy*, you've probably developed a few aches and pains of your own. Perhaps this is another reason why we like dogs so much. Dogs can't talk, so they can't tell us when they feel bad or how bad they feel. Unfortunately, because they can't tell us how they are feeling, we may miss the signs of illness. And in this case, we really do want to know.

The Loving Touch

One of the best ways to tell if your dog is healthy is to do what a veterinarian does and touch him. Running your hands along your dog's body can quickly tell you a lot about your dog's overall condition. For starters, it can tell you if he's too thin or too fat. If your dog's sides feel like you could put thimbles on your fingers and play his ribs like a washboard, then he's too thin (though some breeds, like greyhounds and salukis, are naturally svelte). If, on the other hand, you can't feel his ribs at all, your pup is a porker and needs to lose some weight.

Regular grooming is the best way to notice any changes. It's also a great way to bond with your pet as well as keep his coat in top condition and reduce shedding. As you groom him, feel for any new lumps or bumps. Are there any sores or unusual swellings on your dog's body? Feel your dog's abdomen and along his spine for areas of any pain. How does his coat look? Is it free of mats and fleas or ticks? Does his coat look shiny and silky or is it dull and lifeless? Are there bald patches that could indicate a skin disease? Look for rashes that could signal your dog has allergies. Check between his toes, too, for foxtails or other paw problems. When you pull on your dog's skin, does it snap back like a rubber band? If not, your dog could be dehydrated.

The Tail End

Forgive me for being indelicate, but do you know the scoop on your dog's poop? If you pick up after him, as you should, then you are aware of an obvious health indicator—his bowel habits. Are his stools firm or runny? Are tapeworm segments, blood, or mucous present? There can also be other trouble brewing in the end zone. Check the anal sacs on either side of the dog's anus. They need to be emptied to avoid infection. Usually, the sacs empty naturally whenever the dog defecates, but if they don't they can become so infected that they must be removed entirely. Be warned: Voiding the anal sacs is an unpleasant, stinky task you may prefer to leave to your veterinarian, but no matter who does it, your dog will thank you in the end.

Eyes, Ears, Nose, and Throat

They say the eyes are the mirrors of the human soul. I maintain that the eye of the dog mirrors a purer soul. The dog's eyes are also the mirror of their health status. If your dog's eyes are clear, bright, and alert, that means he's probably in good overall health.

Have you smelled your dog's ears lately? An unpleasant odor could indicate an infection. While your dog is lending you an ear, also check the insides for redness or ticks, as this is a favorite dining spot for these pesky little bloodsuckers.

The nose knows whether your dog is feeling up to snuff, or sniff. A moist nose is a healthy dog's nose. A dry, cracked nose, especially if accompanied by mucous, is a warning sign of illness.

Check your dog's throat area for any signs of swelling or pain. Pressing around his windpipe should not cause him to cough.

Is Flossy Flossing?

A sure sign of tooth trouble in people or dogs is bad breath, and regular dental care is just as important for your dog as it is for you. Take a whiff of your dog's breath. If it smells fresh, that's good, but if it's worse than your gym socks after a week in the laundry hamper, it's time for a doggie dental checkup. Chances are that you'll discover your dog's teeth have a buildup of tartar that your veterinarian should remove. Check your dog's gums, which should be firm and pink, never red or bleeding. Also check for missing or broken teeth. Your canine should always have his canines—the better to chew biscuits with, my dear.

Valley of the Dogs

A man and his dog walk into a psychiatrist's office. The dog climbs up on the couch, and for once no one tells him to get down. The psychiatrist takes out his pad and pencil and says to the dog, "Just lie back and relax."

The dog circles three times and lies down.

"Now, Rex, tell me what seems to be the trouble."

"Well, Doc, it's like this," Rex says with a sigh. "I'm tired of living the domestic life."

The psychiatrist keeps scribbling notes on his pad. "Yes, go on. I'm listening."

"I long to be free. I want to unleash my inner pup."

"And why can't you do that, Rex?"

Rex points to his master and says, "Because this guy keeps leading me on."

Dogs on the Couch

Have you ever wondered what life must be like for dogs at the end of a leash, following us around all the time? They never get to sniff everything they want to or mark as many hydrants as they'd like. It's like window-shopping from inside a moving car. We decide when and where dogs go, even when they eat and sleep. If we're not dragging them around on a leash, we leave them alone for hours on end to lie around the house just watching their hair shed. It's enough to make a dog downright depressed. Could Prince be popping Prozac? Is Rex ready for Ritalin? In the Valley of the Dogs, it may take pills to cure your canine's ills.

Seriously, dogs can suffer from emotional problems, much the same as we do, some of them more serious than others. The reason for these problems may be that they spend so much time around human beings. By treating our dogs more like people, we can be setting them up for trouble. If your canine is conflicted, he may require the intervention of an animal behaviorist to determine what's biting him or, worse, why he's biting you or other people. Most of the behavioral and emotional problems that plague dogs and cause their owners such woe are simply the result of a lack of basic training and properly establishing the order of the pack.

Top Dog Versus Underdog

Who's top dog in your house? If it's not you, chances are that somebody in the house needs some training, and that's probably you. People who work at animal shelters where millions of dogs (and cats) are surrendered each year say that there are no pet problems, only people problems.

Sadly, we are the root cause of most of our dogs' behavior problems. That occurs either through bad breeding practices like the ones in puppy mills that supply the Little Pet Shops of Horrors or through our failure to give our dogs good training at the outset. Difficult or dangerous dogs are the result of owners who, in a dog's eye view, have not properly established the "me boss, you dog" social status in the household.

From the dog's perspective, you're both members of the same pack, and there can be only one leader. The concept of social rank is deeply ingrained in dogs, and they need to know who is in charge at all times. Ambiguity about lead dog status would never occur in the wild; when it happens at home, your dog learns she can exhibit beastly behavior and get away with it. At the very least, this unsociable behavior helps create bored dogs, as you are less likely to take your dog with you to dog parks or other public places where she might find more constructive ways to entertain herself than demolishing your house, engaging in excessive barking, or doing other undesirable things that end up with her chained to a doghouse in your backyard.

Of course, sometimes a dog is just plain wacko from the get-go. If your Lab is a candidate for a lobotomy and you're about ready to fly over the cuckoo's nest because of your crazy dog, you may need to summon those men and women in white jackets with treats and clickers in their pockets who are experts at rehabilitating difficult dogs and their owners.

A Dog's Eye View

Perhaps we should all spend a little more time following our dogs around and studying their behavior. If we put ourselves in their place more often, we could probably learn a lot from our four-legged friends about being better human beings and more fully enjoying life.

If people followed their dog's example, we might learn to enjoy things like the following:

- Having a good roll in the grass and not worrying about grass stains
- Playing tug of war and letting the other guy win
- Taking frequent naps, even when the boss is looking
- Taking time to stop and sniff the roses (but not pee on them)
- Wiggling our whole bodies when we're happy and not worrying about who's watching
- Living life fully in the moment, because we don't own a watch and can't tell time anyway

Maybe if we knew what it's *really like* to be living a dog's life, we'd all become better dog owners and there'd be no more bored dogs. In the meantime, the rest of this book offers a broad assortment of ideas to make your canine busier and happier. Have fun!

PART 2

Let the Games Begin

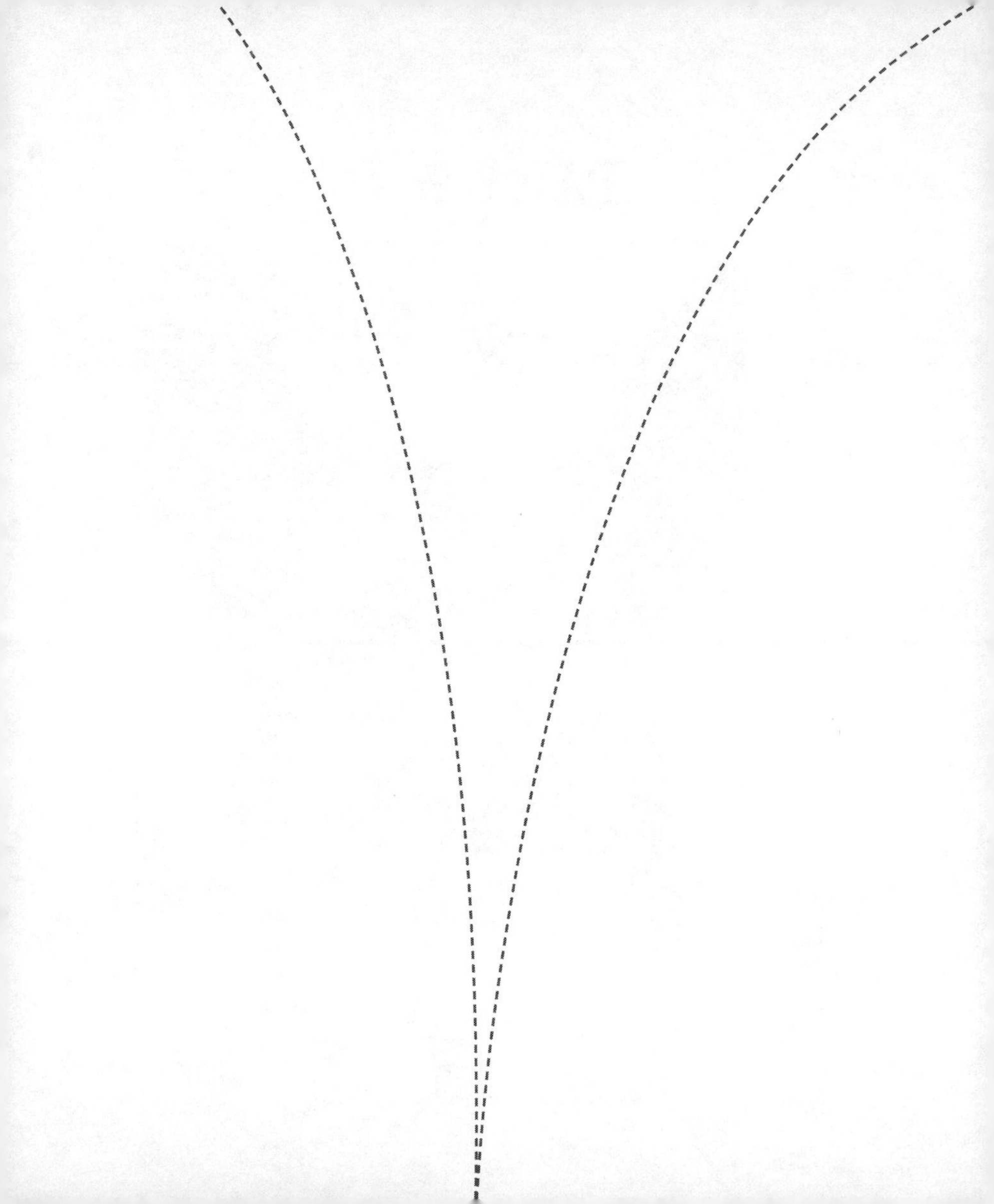

Chapter 6

FUN FUR ONE

If you come home to discover your dog has been stacking up his bone collection like a house of cards, it could mean that he needs a lot more stimulation than you're currently providing for him in your absence. If you're stuck for ideas on how to entertain your dog when he's home alone, this chapter may give you a fresh perspective on the problem. Herein are selections of activities that are fun for one.

Auto-Fetch

If tennis pro Boris Becker had a dog, he'd probably use this device to pitch tennis balls to Bowser Becker. Your dog will be kept busy with this hands-free ball-launching device, the high-tech way to play fetch when you're too busy (or too lazy) to toss a ball. You can set the launcher to pitch the balls at preset intervals, or you can set it to launch a single ball at the press of a button. Just don't be surprised if your Lab develops a winning backpaw and lobs a few balls back at you. In this game of tennis, "love" is the best possible score.

 Hide the Treats

You don't have to dress up like the Easter Bunny for this game (unless you want to, of course). It's kind of like an Easter egg hunt without the reeking rotten eggs you discover hidden under the sofa a month later. Just select some of Fido's favorite treats and hide them in unusual spots. Thinking of good hiding places can be almost as much fun for you as sniffing them out will be for your dog. The more challenging the hiding place, the longer it will take to find, which will help him to better pass the time. You can also time your dog on his treasure hunt to test your dog's smarts. Of course, when you're hiding the treats, you may want to avoid the kitty snack tray, otherwise known as the litter box, or there could be some confusion for your dog as to which treat you meant for him to have.

 Toy Box

Kids have toy boxes; why shouldn't your dog? After all, he's your fur kid. A toy box or basket stocked and regularly replenished with a variety of his favorite toys and treats can keep your dog happily engaged for hours. It's good to rotate the assortment and not provide too many toys at once. Dental chews and toys that don't get consumed too quickly are best.

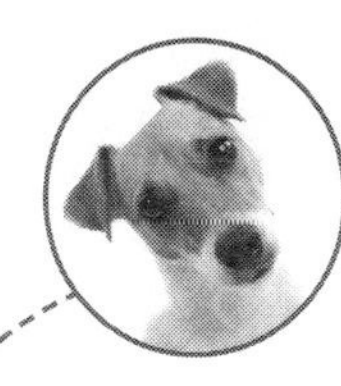

Warning: *Be sure that none of the items you leave could pose a choking hazard. Toys with squeakers could be dangerous if the toy gets torn apart and the dog swallows the squeaker. This is especially a concern with pups and young dogs. Rope toys can also pose a hazard if they shred too easily. It's probably best to supervise your dog with a new toy to be sure he'll be okay when left alone with it.*

Match the breed to the need. Some dogs are also more vigorous chewers than others.

Certain toys are better entertainment for certain types of dogs. For example, an electronic ball launcher might not be the best choice of activity for a basset hound, who might chase one or two balls then go back to snoring on the sofa.

Toys R Fun

There may not be a doggie Toys R Us, but dogs are a lot like kids. They also enjoy having a variety of toys to play with. Irene Culver keeps her Lhasa apso, Toby, entertained by regularly replenishing his stash of stuffed toys. "I think new toys are essential," she says. "Just like people, dogs get bored." It's amazing how your dog's interest will be sparked by the addition of a new toy to his collection.

Yard Sale Toys

Buying a selection of toys for your dog doesn't have to be costly. My mother and I both buy toys for our dogs at yard sales. It's fun searching for the toy you know your dog will love to play with. You can often save a lot of money on brand-new toys this way. Be sure to choose toys that are safe and don't have buttons or other things that can be chewed off and swallowed. Some dogs are more inclined than others to tear toys apart, so keep that in mind when choosing toys at yard sales. Rule of thumb: If they're baby safe, they're probably also dog safe. As Irene Culver says about her dog, Toby, "I pick up small stuffed toys, often with squeakers inside, at yard sales. He's waiting at the door for them!"

Toby's Toy Tug

Sometimes dogs need to be crated for a period of time, such as when traveling or when their owners need a time out. Spending time in a crate can be pretty boring for a dog, but there are ways to make his crate time more entertaining. Irene Culver has a method of keeping her dog, Toby, entertained while he's in his crate. "I stick a dozen toys in the top of his crate so he has to pull and pull them to get them out. Lots of times he will spend several minutes doing that."

Video Dog

If your dog is a couch potato who loves watching TV, he may enjoy watching Animal Planet, nature programs, or some of the new videos and DVDs that are produced especially for bored dogs. *The Dog Sitter,* for instance, is available through *www.pawshop.com*. These videos include the kinds of things that dogs might enjoy watching in real life, such as other dogs, cats, and even birds. They include training tips and sounds that appeal to a dog's sensitive hearing. Unless he's watching *Lassie Come Home* or some other canine classic, your dog may find that these Fido films don't have much of a plot. But he probably won't mind, just as long as he isn't expected to write a review for *Rolling Bone* or nominate any of the four-legged stars for a Patsy Award. If he could, though, he'd probably give them Two Paws Up. Oh, and don't forget the snacks.

Star Search

Is your dog a frustrated star? Is she dying to have her fifteen minutes of fame? Well, why not give it to her. With your help, she can star in her own video to watch any time she's bored. Wendy Kowalewsky says her golden retriever, Chelsea, loves to watch herself on video. "The first few times she sat directly in front of the TV watching, then she would go get the toy that she was playing with on the TV and play with it a bit." One good thing about dog stars is that they'll never let it go to their head or demand outlandish fees for an appearance. They don't have to be good actors, either. There are plenty of actors on TV that aren't very good, but they still get paid lots of money.

A Little Mutt Music

I don't know whether Mozart had a mutt, but his music hath charms to soothe just about anyone, including your bored dog. If you asked a dog what kind of music he prefers, he probably wouldn't choose heavy metal, unless it was the metallic sound of the lid opening on a full garbage can, music to any dog's ears. I've found my dogs seem to be more into easy listening, but then bassets are into just about anything that's easy, and they definitely have ears for music. You can have your dog's favorite music set on a timer to come on intermittently during the day.

Her Master's Voice

If your dog is like the RCA Victor dog, she loves to hear the sound of her master's voice. Hearing your voice while you're away may be the best way to keep your dog happy. Have some fun and get creative when taping your voice. Read a book or just talk to your dog in the loving way you do when you are present. Tell her exactly how you feel about her. She'll love that! My dog, Daisy, loved it when I sang to her, and I had special songs she loved to hear that have her name in them. Even if your singing is like nine-inch nails (no, not the rock group) on a blackboard, there's nothing your dog longs to hear more than the sound of your voice, and she'll enjoy hearing it while you're away. Good thing Apple invented the iDog.

 Rex-ercise

A tired dog is not a bored dog. The best way to ensure that your dog isn't bored when he's alone is to make sure he gets plenty of exercise when you are together. Walk him for an hour a day or let him play at the dog park to help burn off some excess energy. It's also beneficial in keeping him fit and trim. Hey, it's not so bad for you, either!

 Sniffing Out Serenity

Has your dog discovered his comfort zone? You can help soothe your anxious dog with the Comfort Zone Plug-Ins. The same people who came up with plug-in home deodorizers now market aromatherapy plug-ins for your pet. As with the room-freshening variety, the plug-ins heat up and emit pleasing aromas; in this case, the scents use pheromones (those come-hither chemicals whose subtle scent attracts the opposite sex) to make them especially pleasant to a dog's nose. If you didn't know better, you'd say your vizsla was on Valium. It's hard to say whether the Comfort Zone Plug-In smells as good as the neighbor's poodle, but coming home to a calm dog and serene scene is definitely heaven scent.

 Rubdown for Rover

People aren't the only ones who can benefit from a relaxing massage. Dogs love a good rubdown, too, and it's just as soothing for them as it is for you. Start at the tips of the ears, rubbing them gently between your thumb and forefinger. With two fingers, move on to work in circular motions down the length of the dog's body, following the direction in which the hair grows. Don't forget to massage the legs and paws. My dog loved for me to stroke her "palm," the soft, scooped area just behind her paw. Some dogs have spots they don't like touched and others they do. Finish up by stroking his tail, assuming he has one. Giving your dog a massage can be as calming and relaxing for you as it is for him. He won't pay you $60 an hour for your massage therapy services, but he'll love you forever. Actually, he'll love you forever whether you massage him or not.

 Zen Dog

Help your dog achieve Zen in her den with herbs and other calming aids, which you can find at specialty pet stores or your local health food store. Some are also good for soothing human emotions such as stress or even grief. Clomicalm and

Rescue Remedy are two of the more popular herbal remedies for your pet's separation anxiety. Just add a few drops to your dog's water bowl. If you're feeling a little stressed about leaving your dog home alone, rub a little Rescue Remedy on your wrist and you and your dog can zone out together. Play some meditation music and it's Om, sweet Om.

King Kong

No, I don't mean the big hairy ape, but the popular rubber dog-treat-dispenser toy of the same name. The Kong comes in all shapes and sizes to accommodate the tastes of every dog, from Chihuahua to Great Dane. You can purchase treats made especially for dispensing from the Kong, or you can layer it with your own selection of goodies. If your dog is too adept at emptying a Kong, you can make it more challenging for him by varying the sizes and kinds of treats inside; if your dog is less determined and loses interest quickly, make emptying the Kong less challenging for him. Once you've stuffed the Kong, a dollop of cream cheese or peanut butter over the opening will keep the treats from falling out and give your dog an extra taste treat. Maybe they could have coaxed King Kong down from atop the Empire State Building if only they'd had a banana-filled Kong.

Treat and Train

The way to a dog's heart and head is through her stomach. What better way to entertain a dog and motivate her to correct unwanted behaviors than with Treat and Train? This interactive device not only dispenses treats while you're away, it also trains your dog to reward herself for good behavior. If Fifi is a foodie, this gastronomical gizmo is a must-have. Using a selection of games that use tones to cue the dog's behavior, you can teach your dog basic commands like sit, lie down, and stay. You can also teach her to perform all kinds of clever tricks you probably never thought your dog could do. It also can help socialize a puppy. Treat and Train can even be used to reduce unwanted behaviors such as excess barking and chasing the mail carrier. While the Treat and Train is not cheap, owners have found it to be an invaluable tool in keeping bored dogs entertained and are finding new uses for it above and beyond the instructional DVD that comes with the unit.

Smear Tactics

How many times have you bought a new toy for your dog only to have him turn his nose up at it and walk away? To pique your ho-hum hound's interest in a new toy, coat it generously with some cheese spread, peanut butter, or cream cheese (my Daisy's favorite bagel shmear) to make it more interesting and tasty. Also, playing fetch with the new toy a few times will leave your scent on it so your dog will associate the toy with having fun with you.

Health tip: *If you give your dog treat-dispensing toys filled with goodies, like Kongs, the Buster Cube, and Roll-a-Treats, be sure to compensate for the extra calories he's consuming by reducing his food intake at mealtimes and increasing his exercise.*

Ball Bobbing

This is another game for water-loving dogs that don't mind getting a little wet behind the ears—or all over. It's kind of like the children's traditional Halloween game of bobbing for apples. Fill a tub or a child's wading pool with water and add balls or other floating toys for the dog to grab out of the pool. If your dog is a good swimmer, you can add the toys to your swimming pool for him to retrieve. Some dogs will even dive to the bottom to collect their toys. It's also a great way for your dog to keep cool on a hot summer day. Even if he gets tired of bobbing for toys, he can always dog-paddle or lounge on a floating mattress. Just be sure to apply sunscreen to his belly so he doesn't get sunburned.

Wiener Dog Dip

If the ball bob game didn't do it for your Big or Little Dipper, here's something that is sure to get your dog bobbing like crazy. Cut up some hot dogs in bite-sized pieces and put them in a tub or wading pool filled with water. You can also use Vienna sausages. How about polska kielbasa? Heck, any wiener is a winner as far as your dog is concerned. This is also a great game to include if you ever decide to host a Dogtoberfest. Dachshunds can also join in the fun. Just don't let the dogs get confused about which wiener dogs they're supposed to be dipping for.

Pupsicles

Freezing treats is another great way to cool your dog down on a hot day and keep her busy for quite a while, licking away at her favorite flavored pupsicle. And she doesn't even have to chase after the ice cream truck to get these treats. You can freeze beef bouillon, chicken broth, peanut butter, or even

Happy Tail Ale, the new nonalcoholic beer for dogs, if your dog appreciates a good frosty brew while watching you mow the lawn. You can also freeze her favorite treats inside the pupsicles for an extra surprise. Another tasty treat is a rope toy dipped in something yummy and frozen. Frozen treats are also a great remedy for teething pups. If your dog could talk, she'd say, "This is really cool!"

 Tetherball Tug

If your dog is crazy about playing with balls, he might enjoy a rousing game of tetherball with you, your kids, or even himself. If you don't have a tetherball pole in your yard, you can also suspend a rope and tetherball from a tree branch for just as much fun. Jumping up and batting the ball back and forth will keep your dog entertained and also give him a great workout, although you may find you end up with a blowout when he grabs hold of the ball and won't let go. You could also have one very dizzy dog.

 Pup Psychic

Have you ever wondered what your dog is really thinking? You can enlist the services of a pet psychic (or an animal communicator, as they prefer to be called) to help you better understand your dog's inner dialog and why she does the things she does. You can even address your pet's physical and emotional issues. Some work on site, and others don't even have to be present to communicate with your dog. Either way, these pet professionals can divine all kinds of useful information about your dog that will help you better understand her. Finally, you'll be able to find out the answers to important questions, like why Rex keeps humping your leg and where Roxie hid your other tennis shoe.

Stinky Sock Doll

Your stinky socks might smell pretty bad to you, but they smell like heaven to a dog who's missing your di-stink-tive scent. You may remember making sock dolls or sock monkeys when you were a child. You can also make a sock doll or monkey for your dog to play with—stinky or not, your choice. Instead of buttons, which might be swallowed, use permanent colored markers to draw the face. A sock simian is a great toy for when your dog wants to monkey around.

Tip: Leave your socks with your dog while he's convalescing at the animal hospital. It's like having a piece of home there with him and can even help him heal quicker.

 Pop Goes the Bubble!

Lawrence Welk had a bubble machine, and so can your dog. You've probably seen these instant fun makers at kids' birthday parties. Just pour in the special bubble-making potion, turn on the machine, and watch the fun begin. This is also a great way to entertain an energetic dog like a terrier or any other breed that loves to chase things. You might find the whole family joining in the fun. You can rent a bubble machine at most children's toy stores, or you can buy one of the manual bubble-blowing kits and make your own bowser bubbles. All you need now is an accordion player, and your dog will think this game is "wunnerful-a, wunnerful-a."

 Do the Roomba

I'm not suggesting your dog compete in ballroom dance on *Dancing with the Stars,* although some dogs are getting pretty footloose these days in dog dancing. The Roomba is the newest high-tech robotic device that vacuums your floors and frees you up for activities that don't suck quite as much as housecleaning. The Roomba can also be used to entertain your dog in clever ways. My dogs love the vacuum cleaner game, in which I chase them around the room with my vacuum cleaner, but my Hoover doesn't sneak up on them quite like the Roomba can. Just as the Jetsons' dog, Astro, had to learn to stay out of the way of Rosie the robotic maid, this automated room-roving device has no doubt surprised more than a few unsuspecting canines. You can make the Roomba more fun for your dog and keep him entertained by attaching his favorite toy or a cup of treats to the top. He'll keep himself busy chasing after the Roomba and trying to catch his goodies. It's best to indulge your dog with this activity during times when you're in the room, to make sure your dog isn't following Roomba into any tight spaces where he could get stuck or injured.

Demolition Doggie

When I was a kid, I used to wonder what a rumpus room was. Better yet, what's a rumpus? Like your kids, your dog may need his own space where he can go to for a time-out when he's having a tear-able, no-good, very bad day. Perhaps it's a patio add-on, an extra bedroom, or some other area you don't care about getting a little messy. Put your old cast-off sofa or an old chair in it. Your scent will be on the furniture, which will comfort Fido. Stock the room with your dog's favorite toys, old pillows, or what-have-you for a good rip and tear session (especially good for tear-iers). When you come home after a terrible, no good, very bad day at the office, you may even decide to join Rover in that rip-and-tear session for some much-needed stress relief.

Doggie in the Window

We all know the old song, but the question the refrain should have posed was "How *happy* is that doggie in the window?" Can you imagine living in a house with no windows? That would be pretty dull, wouldn't it? Well, your dog enjoys having a window on the world as much as you do. He likes to see who's going past the house, who's coming up the walk, and it's as much for your benefit as it is for his to be able to see who's out there. There's no better crime deterrent than a barking dog, and the size of the dog behind the bark doesn't seem to matter. If he's a big dog that a potential intruder can see through a window, all the better. Provide your dog access to a window while you're away so he can watch the birds, the neighbor's dogs or cats, the neighbor's kids, and the big, busy, fascinating world outside his home.

 Pup Porthole

A neighbor of ours has a very effective way of keeping their hyperactive wirehaired terriers entertained during the day. They cut two circular portholes in their fence at dog-viewing height and put Plexiglas over them so the dogs can see out. It created a kind of canine sidewalk construction site, only through these holes the spectators are looking out at the activity, not in. These portholes give a dog another kind of window on the world. Being able to see all the interesting street activity and bark at passersby, both two-legged and four-legged, can keep a dog entertained for hours. It has certainly worked for these two energetic fellows, except that now they argue about who gets to look out which porthole.

 Good Neighbor Fence

Here's another way to provide your dog with a little company in your absence. If your neighbor has a dog, put a Plexiglas window in the fence so the dogs can see each other. Both will be entertained while their owners are out. If the dogs get along well, you could even put in a flap in the fence to let them go back and forth between yards, share their spaces, and play together. Of course, you'll want to be sure that your neighbor keeps his gate locked at all times so your dog can't escape.

 Through the Woofing Glass

Mirror, mirror on the wall, who's the bored-est dog of all? As long as you can fool her into thinking there's another dog in the house, it's probably not your dog. All you need is a full-length mirror so your dog can see herself. Depending on the dog, this activity can keep a lonely dog happily engaged for quite a while. She may not realize right away that the dog in the mirror looks oddly familiar, but she'll probably wonder why it doesn't ever run away when she barks at it. In fact, if your dog tends to be very territorial, this standoff could go on for hours. Of course, if your dog is a narcissist, you'll never be able to get her away from the mirror.

> I once had a poodle named Tuita. As is typical of the breed, Tuita was very smart and not easily fooled. Once, when she encountered her reflection in a freestanding mirror, she became very curious about the strange dog she saw. Reasoning that the dog must be somewhere inside the mirror, she walked around to the back of it to find where

that other black poodle was hiding. Fortunately, she didn't try to leap through the looking glass, like Alice did.

Ding-a-Ling Doggie

One of the most exciting events of a dog's day is when the front doorbell rings. Even when my dogs hear a doorbell on TV that sounds like our own, it's like a pair of greyhounds out of the starting gate at Derby Lane racetrack.

Here's a clever ruse I sometimes use to add a little spice to my dogs' day, and it's also something you can employ in your absence. All you need is a willing neighbor who will come to your door intermittently throughout the day and ring the doorbell. No matter how many times the bell rings, the dogs will always respond the same way. If your neighbor's name happens to be Ivan Pavlov, all the better.

Up, Pup, and Away!

If your dog loves catching and chasing bubbles and isn't afraid of loud popping sounds, he'll think this game is a real gas. Inflate some children's balloons and let your little balloonmeister see how many he can catch and pop. He'll have lots of fun leaping up, up, and away to catch all his beautiful balloons. This game should be supervised to be sure he doesn't swallow any of the balloons. You don't want him ending up in the Macy's Thanksgiving Day parade.

 Water Wiggle Wagger

Water Wiggle, the outdoor water game by Wham-O, was created for kids, but works just as well to cool off your dog on a summer day. In the same way children love running through the sprinklers on a hot afternoon, your water-loving dog will enjoy getting sprayed repeatedly by this squiggly, wiggly water jet game. Just be sure that your dog isn't inclined to chew the jet head or hoses, since they could pose a choking hazard if they come off. Otherwise, turn on the garden hose and let the jets spray away! If you don't want to buy the Water Wiggle, your lawn sprinklers are also good for water dogs on a hot day.

 Dig for Buried Treasure

Ahoy, Matey! The pirate Long John Silver had nothing on your dog when it comes to seeking buried treasure. Some dogs come naturally equipped with the kind of paws that were made for digging, and it's just his doG-given nature to want to use them for shovels. Unfortunately, that digging tendency can be bothersome for some owners when the digging takes place in areas of your yard that you'd prefer it didn't. If you have a dog that loves to dig, here's something he'll *really* dig. Bury an assortment of yummy treats around the yard in areas where you don't mind Digby doing a little excavating. Every canine worth his kibble knows that just about anything tastes better after it's been aged for a while in dirt. Searching for this buried treasure can keep your dog busy for hours. Eureka, he's found it!

Pup Tent

Ah, the great outdoors! There's nothing like it. Like us, our dogs just love getting out into the wide-open spaces to catch a whiff of some fresh air. Wendy Lee's shepherd/Lab mix, Snooper, loved to go camping with her owner. Can't you just picture the thought bubble over your dog's head as the old dogmobile arrives at Camp Bagawagabiskit? He's probably thinking, "Man, just look at all those trees! And they're mine, all mine!" If you have your own beagle scout who loves the woods and the aroma of Alpo cooked over an open flame, you might want to do what Wendy did for her dog. She gave Snooper her own pup tent. "I filled it with her toys, food, water, and bed whenever we camped. She was happy as can be in *her* tent."

 For the Birds

Most dogs would agree that being left alone is for the birds, unless there are birds for the dog to watch. Birdfeeders can attract all kinds of feathered friends for your dog to watch and bark at. Providing nesting boxes for birds is also a good way to keep the birds coming and going all day long while they build their nests and feed their young. Wendy Kowalewsky says, "When my golden retriever, Chelsea, was young, I was very concerned about her being bored while I was gone. I had birdfeeders directly outside the windows so she could watch the birds and occasional squirrel." My neighbor has gone a step further. He has a parrot that talks to his dogs all day.

 Time Is on His Side

Put your TV and radio on a timer whenever you leave the house so that they will come on and shut off intermittently throughout the day. Most dogs prefer to watch Animal Planet or other dog-approved TV stations. Classical music is the most relaxing choice on the radio, although talk radio is also good. That way your dog hears the sound of a human voice while you're gone. You just might not want the voice he hears to be that of Howard Stern, even if it is on the Sirius channel.

Pup Portrait

Throughout the centuries, dogs have inspired artists to try to portray the essence of these devoted creatures that share our lives and capture our hearts. What could be more special than having a treasured portrait of your own dog? There are numerous pet artists you can commission to paint your dog. Just browse the pages of any dog magazine and you'll find artists who advertise their services. Or you might like to explore your creativity and try painting your own dog's portrait. You might even be able to sell your dog art. Now if you can only get Fido to stay still for his sitting.

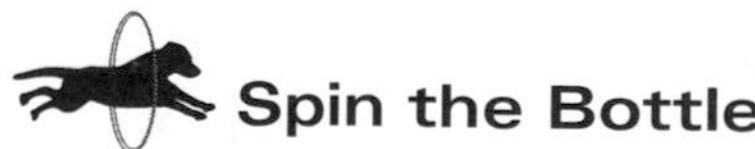

Spin the Bottle

Here's a new twist on an old game of romance that boys and girls used to play together, where the object was to get a kiss. The object of this canine version is to get another kind of treat. Fill an empty plastic water bottle with dog treats and leave the cap off the bottle. Use treats small enough to fit in the bottle but large enough not to come out too easily. Your dog will entertain himself trying to get the treats out of the bottle. If you have two dogs for spin the bottle, they may enjoy playing the game together, but if you come home and find them in the closet playing Post Office, you may have to break it up.

Flipper-ing Out

Most dogs love watching animal shows on TV. If Animal Planet isn't on, you can always choose a channel that is showing an animal movie or TV series. The sounds of barks and meows can pique the interest of a bored dog, but other animal sounds can, too. What about the sound of a dolphin? One can only imagine what a dog would do if he heard those high-pitched chirps and chutters.

Whenever Wendy Kowalewsky has to leave Chelsea in a motel, she turns the television to cartoons, her favorite shows while at home, or animal shows. Once she left Chelsea with the movie *Flipper* playing on TV. Now Chelsea flips out every time she hears the word "Flipper." Wendy discovered a great way to amuse her dog, and she didn't even do it on porpoise.

Sand Trap

What kid doesn't love digging in the sand? What could be more fun than getting sand between your toes? It's no different for your fur kid. They also love the sensation of sand in their dewclaws. If you don't live near the ocean, you can use your kid's sand box for this game that your dog will really dig. And he doesn't even have to score a hole in one. Hide your dog's favorite ball, toys, and a selection of treats in the sandbox. He'll have fun digging in the sand to find the treasures you've buried there for him. Just be sure that the cat hasn't used the sandbox first!

Doggie Bag

You know the looks you sometimes get when dining out in a fancy restaurant after you finish a meal and ask for a doggie bag. The server is thinking, "Yeah, sure. We all know that's for you and not for your dog." When Wendy Kowalewsky goes to a restaurant and asks for a doggie bag, it's no lie.

It's definitely for a doggie. Whenever she comes back from having a meal out, she always brings Chelsea her own doggie bag. Wendy says, "This is a very special treat because she normally doesn't get people food." Chelsea thinks that's the dog's dinner!

Pup Parcel

In *The Sound of Music,* Maria sings about brown paper packages tied up with strings being one of her favorite things. When I was a kid there was nothing I loved more than receiving a parcel in the mail wrapped in brown paper. You couldn't help wondering what wonderful surprise was inside the package. If your dog is anything like mine, she will also love surprise packages. Wrap up some of your dog's favorite treats or a tempting chewy for her to unwrap. If it's Christmastime, you can even use gift wrap paper and tell her Santa Paws left it under the tree. Make sure it isn't too hard for her to open but just challenging enough to keep her busy for a while. She may even be so engrossed in opening her surprise that she'll forget all about barking at the postal carrier or the meter reader for the day. Make sure to supervise your dog while she's opening her gifts so she doesn't eat the paper!

An Apple a Day

To get to the core of a dog's boredom, just peel him an apple. My dogs love apples and they are a healthy, low-fat snack. An apple a day keeps the doctor and boredom away, at least for some dogs. Wendy Kowalewsky's dog, Red, found a way to keep himself entertained with apples. She says that Red slept and ate in the house, but if he was outside and decided he was hungry, he'd go to the apple trees. Once in the orchard, he'd stand on his hind legs and pick a couple of apples to munch on. They may have even been Washington Reds, since that's the state where Wendy lives.

Rubik's Tube

There are lots of things you can do with an empty gift-wrap tube, and with a little imagination some of them can help entertain your dog. Here's an idea. Fill an empty gift-wrap tube with small dog biscuits or some tasty treats. Tape up one end so the biscuits don't fall out too easily. Leave the other end open. The treats will rattle around inside the tube and make the game more interesting. See if your dog can figure out how to get all the treats out of the tube. If he turns out to be really good at this game, perhaps you can persuade him to do all your gift-wrapping next Christmas.

Room for One More

Sometimes all your lonely, bored dog needs to be content is the company of another canine, or even a cat. Here's a way that you can keep your dog entertained and also help a pet in need: foster. Providing a temporary haven for homeless pets is a wonderful way to make life more interesting for your dog and give an orphaned dog or cat a second chance at a happy life.

Rescue organizations are in constant need of foster homes for the thousands of pets surrendered each year at pounds and shelters. Of course, you wouldn't want to bring home another pet if you can't give it all the love and attention it deserves, and many foster pets do have special needs. Also, be certain that your dog will accept a new roommate. If you can provide what is required for one of the many homeless pets in need of a loving sanctuary, then by all means make room for one more. But be warned, you could fall in love and become a foster flunkie.

 Pea-nutty

Most dogs go simply nutty over peanut butter. It's the best way to slip your dog a pill without his knowing it, and it's also a great way to keep him from being bored. If you've ever seen the TV ad for milk where the little boy gives his dog a spoonful of peanut butter, you know that a glob of gooey peanut butter can keep a dog busy licking for quite a while. Dru Dunham uses peanut butter to keep his dog happily entertained. He says, "I place peanut butter in a rubber Kong and freeze it. It takes my greyhound, Seth, hours to get all the peanut butter."

 Dog and Mouse

You hear a lot about cats getting on the computer, usually while their owners are trying to work at the computer. They are always lounging around on the keyboard and batting at the mouse, of course. Some dogs have also been known to be quite computer literate. One dog even managed to send an e-mail while his owner was away from the computer. Dru Dunham says, "I leave my computer on so Seth can order dog toys and greyhound coats during the day." From some of the strange e-mails I get, I have to wonder what my dogs are doing at the computer when I'm not there.

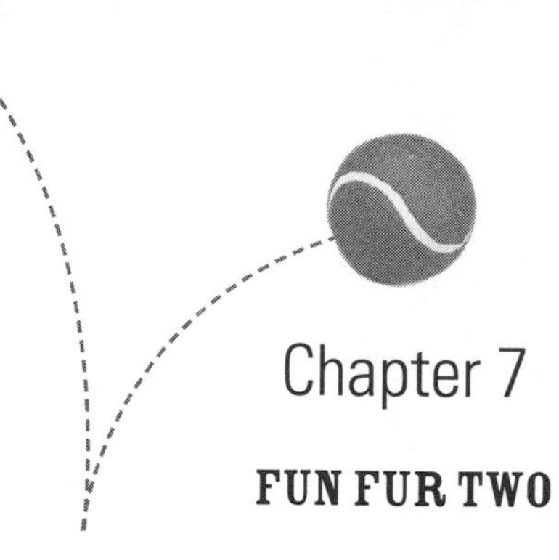

Chapter 7

FUN FUR TWO

Two is always twice the fun, especially when it comes to ensuring that your dog is having quality time and avoiding mind-numbing, tear-the-house-down boredom. Just knowing that you are in close proximity is enough to keep your dog from having separation anxiety, but it's not always enough to keep her from being bored out of her skull. Just ask any writer's dog. Lying around the house all day doing nothing can be pretty boring for your dog, even when she's not alone. Here are some fun activities for you and your dog that are sure to spark up her day—and yours, too!

Hanging Eight

If your active, athletic dog is bored, you could try giving him a board—a skateboard, that is. Some dogs have been known to create their own brand of canine fun by hanging eight on a skateboard. You might first have to give him a few lessons in sidewalk surfing before he can keep the board moving on his own. But if he gets the hang of it, he'll not only keep himself entertained for hours, he could end up being one cool skating doggie dude with the neighborhood kids. Of course, this game might not work as well if you have a belly dragger like a dachshund or a basset hound, since the dog's feet should be able touch the ground. Fortunately, a skateboard also makes a swell come-along for a short-legged dog.

Bungee Jumping

Remember when you used to put your toddler in a jumper seat to keep him or her entertained while you were busy? There's a similar way for keeping a bored dog from bouncing off the walls. If your canine just loves to play leap dog, here's something that will keep him jumping for joy. Attach his favorite toy to a long, strong elastic cord like a bungee cord (being sure to remove the hook on the end so your dog won't be injured). He'll have a ball leaping up again and again to try and catch the toy. Once he latches on, he'll have so much fun bouncing around at the end of the bungee cord, he'll think he's on a thrill ride at a Six Wags theme park.

 Shell Game

Here's a sideshow barker's trick you can play on your dog. You can even test his intelligence with this different take on the old carnival shell game. Upturn some empty containers like Tupperware or cereal bowls, and hide a scrumptious treat under one of them. Don't let your dog see which container you choose. That would be cheating. Make sure he doesn't peek; blindfold optional. Give him the command, "Find it!" See how long it takes for your dog to figure out where you've hidden the treat. If you have a stopwatch, you can time your dog's ability to topple the container and find the treat that's hidden there. Now, if you can get your clever dog to hide a treat for you to find, you two are definitely ready for the David Letterman show.

 Limbo Unleashed

Here's a popular party game you can play with your dog. Suspend a pole at varying heights going from highest to lowest and see if you and your dog can slip under the pole together without dislodging it. You may need to coax your dog with a treat to join you in this game, or he may surprise you by showing how low he can go. Once he gets the idea, he can try it solo. Be sure to reward him and make a big fuss when he goes under the pole without knocking it down. Oh, and don't forget to play "The Limbo Rock" by Chubby Checker while you are playing this game to make it more fun. This is also a great activity for several dogs. How low can you go?

Pole Vault

How high can your dog jump? If you've ever wondered, you can play that last game in reverse by seeing how high your dog can jump over the pole. Start at the lowest point where you left off in Limbo and gradually raise the pole higher and higher to see how high your dog can leap over the pole. He may surprise you with his vaulting ability. This is also great practice if you're training your dog for an agility competition. On the other hand, if you have a short-legged dog like a basset hound or dachshund, you may want to just leave the pole where it was and forget the whole thing.

Dogs at Work

Times have changed in the workplace, and so have attitudes toward bringing dogs to work. More and more companies are encouraging people to bring their pets to work (and I don't just mean dogs). While not every business encourages canines in the cubicle, rules in many companies have relaxed toward permitting dogs at work, as long as they are well behaved and potty trained, of course. This is largely because the bean counters at the top of the chain finally figured out that happy employees are productive employees, and that if people can have their pets with them while they work, then they are happier spending eight hours a day there. Why, they might even whistle while they work, but if they do, an unusually furry, four-legged staff member will probably answer that whistle.

 What Color Is Your Pup's Parachute?

Is your dog living up to his full potential? If not, that could be why he's bored. He may have untapped talent that needs to be put to good use. A busy dog is a happy dog. Maybe your dog isn't a stay-at-home hound but is instead a career canine at heart. He may need a little career counseling or perhaps a good trainer to find out what he's best at doing. You might even want to call in a pet communicator or a dog whisperer. Maybe with their help your dog will tell you exactly what he wants to do with his life.

A big hint is to consider what your dog was bred to do. If he's a mutt, what is the predominant breed in his bloodline? If you have a scent hound that's good at sniffing out just about anything or a breed that has a strong retrieving instinct, you might have a dog that could be trained in search and rescue or even police work. If you have a gentle soul who's good with people, he might make a great therapy dog. If your dog is kept busy with work, he won't be spending nearly as much time alone and bored. He might be so good at his job that he even gets a promotion before you do!

Alpohorn

You don't have to dress up in Tyrolean garb for this (unless you want to, of course). You also don't have to live in the Swiss Alps or know how to play the alpenhorn. Using an empty gift-wrap tube, make loud bellowing noises into it and watch your dog's reaction. (If you live where there are moose or yak herds, you might not want to do this outdoors during rutting season.) I've never seen a dog yet that didn't find this game exciting and bark like crazy at the other end of the tube. If you're wearing lederhosen, you've had some schnapps, and your dog has had some Happy Tail Ale, then you both can enjoy a slaphappy Dogtoberfest together.

 Tucker's Treat Trick

Lynda Marenich says, "We have a husky-shepherd mix named Tucker who is very smart and misses living in her wilderness on the coast. When we moved back to the city, my son came up with a great trick to keep her entertained. Tucker is instructed to lie down, and then a treat is put on top of her paw. She was taught to wait until released to eat the treat, and now you can walk into another room and she will not budge until released. My son learned patience and persistence (not to mention developing an interest in training dogs), and I guess Tucker did, too."

 Sock It to Me!

When it comes to entertaining a dog with something that appeals to his love for all things stinky, you can't beat a good old smelly sock. If it's a week-old sock from your gym locker, that's even better. Here is something else fun for your dog that you can do with just an ordinary sock: a sock on the nose! (No, not that kind of a sock!) My dogs love this game that began with my basset hound Dolly, who loved stinky socks. Even Daisy, who was never a very playful dog, liked it when I slipped a sock on the end of her nose. I got on my hands and knees in a play bow and used my high-pitched play-with-me voice when I was doing this to engage her in the game.

Sometimes she would pull the sock off right away with her forepaws, but more often she patiently waited for me to pull it off. She happily tolerated my sliding it on her snout repeatedly, which is amazing because she didn't tolerate much else coming near it, especially when there was food involved. (The first time I ever tried to take a treat away from her I nearly became a double amputee.) I'm not sure whether it's the pungent aroma of the sock that attracted her or exactly what it was she loved about this silly sock game, but it was one of our favorite games we played together.

Healing Paws

Your dog is not only good at heeling, but he's also good at healing. Just petting a dog can reduce stress, lower your blood pressure, and have other beneficial effects on your health. That's why more nursing homes and hospitals are permitting dogs to visit their patients. The positive outcome of the interaction between dogs and people who are ill or infirm has been well documented, and your dog may be a perfect candidate for such a program. The dog's temperament is, of course, paramount in deciding whether he qualifies to be a therapy dog. He must be gentle, low-key, and enjoy a lot of human contact. If your dog is approved for this kind of work, taking your dog to a senior facility or children's hospital could brighten someone else's day besides your own, and your dog's, too.

Agility Is A-maze-ing!

Agility is just one of the many dog sports that has become popular in recent years. For those who are not yet familiar with it, agility consists of a course that includes various obstacles for dogs to navigate their way over, under, and through. This maze for the mutts can include hurdles, seesaws, and tunnels. There are also many agility-based games, like Snooker, that are enjoyable and challenging for both dog and handler.

Agility competitions that draw many enthusiasts and their four-legged friends are held throughout the country. With practice and patience (yours), your dog can improve his speed and time running an agility course. If you're not the competitive type, you can set up an agility course in your own backyard. It's just as much fun for you and your dog, only without the pressure of competing. People have a tendency to make work out of everything. The main thing here is to just have fun with your dog.

 Dirty Dog Dancing

You don't have to wear a tux to participate in the latest canine freestyle craze, known as dog dancing, but the dogs will already be wearing tails. And in dog dancing, it's okay if your partner has two left feet. Together you can do the tango, mambo, and foxtrot. In bowser ballroom dancing, you and your dance partner are scored according to the technical and artistic elements of your routine. Fancy costumes and that Fred Astaire flair are also important elements of your final score. Who knows, you might soon appear on *Dancing with the (Dog) Stars.* You can learn more about tripping the light fantastic with your dog at *www.caninefreestyle.com.*

I'll Fly Away

Look! It's a bird! It's a plane! No, it's a flyball dog! Attention, all owners of Border collies and other manic mutts: Your dog can't help but burn off some of that excess energy while participating in this popular canine sport. In flyball, your dog races in a relay with three other dogs on a team. They run on a course with four hurdles spaced ten feet apart. Once they leave the starting line, the dogs jump the hurdles and press the lever on a spring-loaded box that fires off a tennis ball. The dog catches the tennis ball and then runs back over the four hurdles. As soon as the dog crosses the starting line, then the next dog continues the relay and so on, until all four dogs have run the course. The first team to complete the course with all four dogs without committing any errors wins the heat. For flyball dogs, life is definitely a ball!

Disc-o Dog

Do you have a Frisbee dog? If you have a Border collie, an Australian shepherd, or one of the legions of adoptable mixes from shelters that are simply dizzy about a disc spinning through the air, then you probably do. There are many clubs and competitions devoted solely to this exciting doggie sport, and there are even special types of Frisbees especially for use in competitions, which are usually made of more pliable (and chewable) plastic than the Frisbee you played with when you were young.

Your dog may or may not show a natural aptitude for the sport, but most dogs can be taught to catch a Frisbee on the fly. While you can't always tell if a puppy will have an interest in chasing a Frisbee, many shelters will let you take a potential adoptee onto a grassy area to see how the dog responds to you and your Frisbee.

Training begins with teaching your dog to fetch an object, bring it back to you, and hopefully drop it on command. You can teach your dog to leap for an airborne disc by first having him spring from off your knee to catch the disc on the fly. With practice, you'll soon have a die-hard disc-o dog.

Pawcasso

Could your dog have creative talent you're not aware of? Judging from some of the creative messes he's made in your house, it could well be the case. You can help your dog discover his inner artist in a more positive, and even profitable, way. All you need is a canvas, some poster paint, four paws, and even a bushy tail instead of a paintbrush. Spread the canvas flat, dip your dog's paws in the paints, and unleash your dog's creative flair. With some training, you can also hold the canvas upright and command your dog to "paint." For all you know he could be the next Jackson Pawlock. Don't laugh. Some pooch paintings can fetch up to $2,000! Be sure to use nontoxic, washable paints, or you may have a blue dog on your hands.

 Roll Out the Bagel

My basset hound Bubba Gump loves to chase mini-bagels (less fattening, for canines watching their carbs). He has a preference for the Sara Lee brand bagels—plain, not flavored, if you please.

(Caution: do not use cinnamon raisin, since raisins are harmful to dogs.)

Here's how the game goes every morning. He barks at me until I roll the bagel across the floor. I must do this repeatedly. He chases after it, catches it on the roll, and flings it across the room like a Frisbee. He has developed a technique any expert Frisbee flinger would envy. I have to fetch the bagel for him and roll it across the floor again and again until he finally tires of the sport and settles down to eat it. It's clear to the casual observer which of us is better trained and who gets more exercise while playing this game. Being a French dog, Bubba also occasionally enjoys a good roll using a croissant or brioche. Bun appetit!

Getting Fit with Fido

People aren't the only ones who develop expanding waistlines and the numerous health problems associated with being overweight, such as heart disease and diabetes. Dogs do, too. Like us, they need regular exercise to keep fit and trim and to maintain a healthy weight. When was the last time you weighed your dog? Hopefully it was at the veterinarian's office because you make sure he gets regular checkups. If your dog has been partaking too often of those bagels, treats, and doggie delicacies from the pawtisserie, he may be putting on some extra pounds. If, like a growing number of Americans, you and your pup are getting a bit too pudgy, here are some exercises you can do with your best friend for fun as well as fitness.

Treadmill Mutt

You may have one of these exercise machines around your house; that is, if it wasn't sold at your last garage sale or hasn't been designated as a closet-expanding clothes hanger. If you have a treadmill, you'll find that both you and your dog can have a good workout on it. Just place Fido beside you on the treadmill, hold onto his leash, and trot away. Make sure that the speed is set at a comfortable level for your dog's size and ability, and don't overexercise him, or yourself, especially if you are just starting out on an exercise regimen. Remember, your legs are longer than his are, so if he's having trouble keeping up or you see obvious signs he's tiring, ease up the pace. If you're both panting and drooling, it's time to step off the treadmill.

Jog-a-Dog

Jogging with your dog is also great exercise. Dogs love to run, but joggers can often get so deep into a runner's endorphin high that they forget that their dogs may not be able to keep up a marathon pace with them. The same advice for the treadmill applies to jogging with your dog. This is another instance where matching the breed to the need is important.

One thing I hate to see is a dog (especially an older dog) running alongside a die-hard jogger, its tongue nearly dragging the ground, obviously exhausted. If you run with your dog, take occasional breaks, particularly if he is a senior. Be considerate of your dog's needs and watch for signs that he might be getting tired. Your dog will run with you until he drops because he wants to please you at all costs, but you don't want that to happen, I'm sure. Stop and let your dog sniff and piddle and do all the things dogs like to do. After all, it's his run, too!

Obviously, if you have a short-legged breed of dog like a basset hound, forget about running marathons or even half-marathons with him. In fact, you can forget about running for any distance with him without making frequent sniff and piddle stops. It's just the nature of the nose hound. Bassets are plodders, not joggers.

Bicycle Built for Two

Many people like to exercise their dogs while riding a bicycle. This can be a good workout for both of you, but again some caution is advised. Some breeds are better suited to this activity than others. While you can exercise your dog by letting her run alongside your bike, keep pace with her rather than thinking she should keep pace with you. It's cruel to expect her to run for miles nonstop.

It's also best to be certain your dog is trained to run alongside your bike and not in front of it. Going head first over the handlebars is not much fun. Don't forget to wear your helmet, just in case she decides to make an unexpected stop along the bike trail. In fact, it's always a good idea to wear your helmet. You never know when someone else's dog may decide to run in front of your bicycle.

A Tisket, a Tasket, a Bowser in Your Basket

There are alternatives to having your dog run beside you on a bike. Toy breeds can ride easily in a handlebar basket, which won't slow you down and will still be fun for you both. Your dog will enjoy the feeling of the wind blowing through his fur as he rides along with you, especially if you reward him for being a good passenger. Your dog can also ride tandem with you in one of the travel trailers made for cyclists with children—or fur children. Riding in a trailer also keeps your dog protected from the sun and elements. He may not get a lot of exercise being a passenger in a bike trailer, but he'll sure be an easy rider. Don't forget to let him out to take occasional potty breaks.

Double Dog Dutch

Perhaps you may remember this jump rope rhyme from your childhood:

> I had a little puppy
> His name was Tiny Tim

I put him in the bathtub to see if he could swim
He drank all the water;
He ate a bar of soap
The next thing you know he had a bubble in his throat.
In came the doctor,
In came the nurse,
In came the lady with the alligator purse
Out went the doctor
Out went the nurse
Out went the lady with the alligator purse.

You might have been singing this rhyme about your puppy back then, but chances are you probably weren't jumping rope with her. Or maybe you were. Either way, it's never too late for a little game of double Dutch with your dog. If your dog is a good jumper and your knees are up to the challenge, why not let her join in the fun and jump rope with you? It's not only a great workout for both of you, but if you keep up this fitness regimen every day, you'll soon be so fit you'll never have to call in the doctor or the nurse. But you might want to call in the lady with the alligator purse, especially if she's carrying dog treats in it.

 Weed-Eater

Wendy Kowalewsky says, "Chelsea loves to help me garden. When I am pulling weeds, I throw them out of the garden. She is right on the job and grabs those weeds, shakes them and tears them apart. She is ready and waiting when the next handful of weeds is thrown. In the fall she expects payment for her work, and if I didn't enclose the vegetable garden she would help herself to the vegetables. She absolutely loves carrots. When I'm canning tomatoes, if I don't keep them out of her reach, she will snitch them. She must figure that is her bonus for destroying all the weeds."

 K-9 Karaoke

No party these days seems complete without a karaoke machine to bring people together in song. But have you ever done karaoke with your dog? If you love karaoke, your dog might like to join you in a duet. Some dogs are just natural vocalizers, so you may not have to coax your dog to sing. Some might need some encouragement, though. If you have a hound dog like I do, you might have to do a little howling of your own, or you might have to gobble like a turkey, as we did for our first basset, Butterscotch, to get her to belt out a few high notes. Anything goes, just as long as you're not planning on trying out for *American Idol.* Simon Cowell would definitely give you the thumbs down on the howl *and* the turkey gobble.

Beam Me Up!

If your dog loves to chase after just about anything that moves, you may be able to help him see the light. A penlight, that is. Turn out the lights in the room and turn on the penlight. Aim it at the wall and make the light dance around all over the room. Watch your dog give chase after the beam for some fun that will help you both lighten up. Chasing a penlight also works with cats. Just don't put the penlight *on* the cat.

Bowlingual Bowser

Is your dog bowlingual? If so, you could teach your dog to "speak" in a different language. If *you* are bilingual, try teaching your dog commands in a different language. Using the same tone of voice you would use for commands in English, teach him to sit, stay, and lie down. You may be surprised how much your dog understands, and he won't be lost in translation on your next trip abroad. Next thing you know he'll be saying "Oui" instead of "Woof!" or he might bid you "Arf wiedersehen" instead of saying goodbye.

Doggie Duet

Can your dog play the piano? Put him on the bench beside you, and place his paws on the keyboard. If you play along, he may try to imitate you. A few well-placed treats may encourage him to join in the duet. Don't expect him to play Chopin right off, though. You may have to start him out practicing some arf-peggios on the ivories. If he starts to croon along with the music, he may soon find himself on *American (Dog) Idol.*

Howling at the Moon

There's just something about a full moon that brings out the animal in you and makes you want to howl at it, even if you aren't a dog. My basset hounds and I love to howl at a full moon, but they're a lot better at it than I am. Here's how to make sure that there's no blue moon for your lonely dog. Next full moon, step outside with your dog and start to howl at the top of your lungs. Your dog probably won't need much encouragement to join in the howlfest. If you live in the city, though, you might want to warn your neighbors so they don't think they're living next door to a lunatic.

Puppy Pilates

You can use your small-breed dog to create extra resistance for the leg lifts in your Pilates workout. (No, I don't mean the kind of leg lifts that your dog does on the neighbor's shrubs.) While lying on your back, tuck your legs to your chest and perch your toy breed atop your lower legs (no Great Danes, please, unless you have quads like Arnold Schwarzenegger and can bench press a couple of hundred pounds). Then do repetitions with Rover by raising and lowering your legs. Do as many repetitions as you can. This will not only strengthen your quads and glutes, but your dog will get a free seesaw ride in the bargain. You can do the same thing with sit-ups by placing your small dog on your chest and raising and lowering your upper body. A happy dog and killer abs are guaranteed with this tailwagger's workout.

 Bend It Like Barkham

Some dogs can do a lot more with a ball than simply chase it. Dogs will sometimes devise their own ball games with a little help from their owners. Using a larger ball when playing with your dog can provide some variety from the usual ho-hum game of fetch. For example, try rolling around a soccer ball or basketball for your dog and see what happens. You may really score points with your best friend. I discovered quite by accident that my dog Daisy loved to play soccer when one day while walking in the park we found a soccer ball. I kicked it and she took off after it, using her chest to bop the ball right back to me. She was very good at it and kept the ball in play for quite some time. Try it with your own dog. You could discover you have a future star player on the Manchester Terrier United team.

 Hide and Seek

Dogs love to play hide and seek. This game employs their scenting and prey pursuit instincts. Wendy Kowalewsky's golden retriever, Chelsea, is a big fan. Sometimes they play outside, but most of the time it's in the house. Chelsea sits in a corner while Wendy hides. Once Wendy's in her hiding spot, she yells, "Find me!" and Chelsea is on the hunt, loping through the house with her tail wagging. After a while Wendy's cat, Peanut, decided he wanted to play, too. Now when they hide they have to take Peanut with them. If they don't, the cat sits nearby and meows so Chelsea knows where they are. When Wendy's nieces and nephews were young, they loved coming over and playing hide and seek with Chelsea and Peanut. Of course, the cat probably never responded to the "Ollie, Ollie, all's in free!"

> Our first basset hound, Butterscotch, was a keen hide-and-seeker. Every time my husband and I came home, I would hide from her. Sometimes I hid in the front closet. Other times I'd hide in one of the bedrooms or behind the sofa in the living room. Each time it was someplace different. My British husband would give the command, "Where's Mummy, Butter?" She loved the challenge of sniffing out my whereabouts, which of course was really no challenge at all for a scent hound like the basset, whose keen nose is second only to the bloodhound's in its scenting ability.

 Pup Pub Crawl

In England, it is not uncommon to see a dog in a public house or pub, as bars are called in the British Isles. In fact, you are just as likely to see a dog lapping up the suds from a saucer as you are to see his owner downing a pint. Here in the United States, this is not the case, although the rules are gradually relaxing about allowing dogs in certain establishments that were previously considered off limits. Health laws still dictate that dogs are not permitted where food is prepared. But in some metropolitan areas, where laws have traditionally been the stiffest, you'll see more dogs dining with their owners al fresco. I don't know about you, but while I'm eating, I'd much rather sit next to a dog than a smoker any day.

 Hula Hounds

You can have a lot of fun with your dog and a Hula Hoop. With a little tasty encouragement, you can easily teach your dog how to jump through the hoop. Hold it vertically and coax him through it with a favorite tidbit. Then praise him like crazy. Repeat this a few times until he gets the hang of it. If he seems reluctant to go through the hoop at first, start out with it at floor level and then gradually increase the distance from the floor. Of course, this game won't work with all breeds. Short-legged dogs can't jump as high as some other breeds can, and forcing them to do so could cause a spinal injury. But dogs that are good at flyball and other airborne sports will love jumping through hoops to please you. Just don't ask them to jump through any flaming hoops. Better leave that to the Tahitian fire dancers.

Leaf Leap

When I was a child, I never missed any opportunity to turn work into play. That included raking the leaves. Every autumn it was my responsibility to rake the leaves, a chore I hated. But my dog, Dusty, helped me to make the job fun. I raked the leaves into a big pile, then I would get Dusty to chase after me. After our game of tag, we both took a running leap into the pile of leaves. I'd toss the leaves at Dusty and try to bury him in the leaves, which he loved. Then I'd rake the stray leaves into a mound, and the game would ensue again until we both tired ourselves out and lay atop the leaves looking up at the clouds together. Ah, if only a child's blissful days with a good dog would never leave.

 Chutes and Ladders

Playgrounds aren't just for the kiddies. Dogs can also have a great time playing on some of the playground equipment you'll find in most public parks. I first discovered this with my basset hound Patience, who loved going down the slide at our neighborhood park. I'd tuck her between my legs and we'd slide down in tandem. Besides the slide, there's the merry-go-round, swings, and ladders to climb. Depending on the size and breed and the dog's personality, certain equipment may work better for some dogs than for others. For instance, a toy breed would be better suited to a ride with you in a kiddie swing.

Some parks have regulations about having pets in the area, so check the rules in your park first. I always took my dogs to the school playground in the summertime when school was not in session, so there was no one around to complain. It goes without saying that you shouldn't let your dog soil the sandbox.

 Take a Hike

Just like us, our dogs love the great outdoors. Fresh air, wide-open spaces, and a gazillion trees to water—what's not to love? There are countless places to explore with your canine companion, and any dog worth two scents is always ready and willing to explore them with you. One of my favorite places to take my dogs is Lake Tahoe. We've hiked many of the trails in the area, and some of my most pleasant memories of Tahoe are the adventures I've had there with my dogs. Now that some of them are gone, it pleases me to think I made their lives richer by exposing them to new vistas. To take a hike with your dogs, you don't even need a pup tent. With just a good pair of hiking boots—you can also get special boots for your dog to protect his feet from rough terrain and the elements—food, and water, you're good to go.

Dog Woods

Dolly and Patti knew when we were going to our cabin at Lake Tahoe. When the duffel bag came out of the upstairs closet and they saw me loading a week's worth of socks and underwear along with nearly everything else I owned, it was a sure sign of exciting adventures ahead for the canine members of our pack.

Lake Tahoe is certainly one of the most beautiful places on Earth, and one of the reasons I set my Beanie and Cruiser mystery series there. Of course, my dogs have also provided me with inspiration for these dog lover's mysteries. To Dolly and Patti, it was the land of a million trees and a virtual smell-o-rama of wild, wonderful scents to sample with their keen basset noses. Our cabin skirts several acres of national forest, which was ever a delight to my bassets and me.

Occasionally, I'd take the dogs for a drive in the car while at Tahoe, which they loved. Our favorite destination was Tallac Historic Site, just a few miles up Highway 89 on the way to Emerald Bay. I'd walk them along the beach that seemed to stretch all the way to majestic Mount Tallac to the west. Tahoe's waters, extending miles away to the hazy mountains of the North Shore, were a watercolor artist's wash of aquamarine, lapis, and indigo. I have so many photos of those wonderful days with Dolly and Patti beside the lake. You never saw two happier dogs than my Tahoe twosome.

Batter Pup!

If your dog is a die-hard ball chaser, like a golden retriever or Labrador retriever, here's an activity that will give you both a good workout. The only equipment you'll need is a bat, a ball, and a baseball diamond at your local park or school. You can practice hitting home runs, and your dog can practice his outfielding. You won't even have to retrieve the home runs you send into the bleachers. Your retriever will do that for you.

Irene Culver says, "My black cocker-poo, Niño, followed me around the house with nothing better to do than bark at the vacuum cleaner until it was time to go to my son Chris's Little League Game. No sooner had I parked at the field than Niño was out of the car and on the diamond, tracking a low ball hit into left field. He caught it and kept running, ball in mouth, heading for parts unknown, with nine little boys chasing him, calling "Niño! Niño! Drop that ball!" Coaches and some of the parents watching from the bleachers began to yell, "Sign him up!"

 Literary K-9

Your dog may not have been to the library lately. She probably doesn't even have a library card, but that doesn't mean she doesn't appreciate a good book now and then. No, I don't mean chewing it. Have you tried reading a book to your dog lately? If not, you may be surprised at how much she enjoys a good story. Granted, it's probably the sound of your voice rather than the words that are pleasing to her ears, and the more animated your voice, the better. You can even play books on tape for her if your voice gives out. This is also a great way to keep her entertained while you're out of the house. If you read to her very often, she just may decide she wants her own library card after all. See Spot run—to the nearest bookstore!

Upstairs, Downstairs

Here's a great cardio workout for you and your dog. If you have a staircase in your home, race your dog up and down the stairs to see who gets to the landing first. You can throw a ball up or down the stairs to encourage him to chase after it. This is not an activity that is generally advised for long-backed dogs like dachshunds or basset hounds, since it could cause spinal disk problems. Also, be sure you don't stumble over the dog on the way downstairs or it could be a short trip.

My basset, Dolly, loved running up and down the stairs in our house. In fact, when I first saw her at Hound Hollow, the basset hound rescue facility where I adopted her, she was dashing up and down the stairs. She was by far the liveliest and most energetic basset I've ever owned. I'm sure the stairway to Heaven was no challenge for Dolly, my little stair-climbing hound.

 The Pawtisserie

Nearly every city in America has a dog bakery for those pastry-loving pooches. Three Dog Bakery has a chain of stores that you can visit, and you can even order their treats online. Of course, it's more fun for your dog if you take her to the bakery with you. The selection of doggie delicacies is as varied as any bakery for humans, and they smell so good you'll want to eat them yourself. Your pet can enjoy biscuits and pupcakes made from wholesome, hypoallergenic ingredients. Some shops even keep treats at dog-sampling level for their four-legged customers. Just don't take your dog to the pawtisserie too often or you'll have to do more of that cardio stair climbing with her.

 Tug of War

Most dogs love to play tug of war with just about anything—toys, ropes, leashes, your underwear. I've had great fun playing tug of war with my dogs, though some more aggressive breeds might not be as well suited to this game. Teaching an already powerful and aggressive dog to be more so is probably not the best lesson in how to play nice. When playing tug of war, it's also wise to be selective about the object used in this game of push-me-pull-you. If you use a slipper or some other item you'd rather not have torn to shreds, your dog will think it's okay to do so, even when you're not playing together. Pups especially love playing tug of war, but don't let him win too often or he'll start thinking he's top dog.

Starbarks

Is your canine into caffeine? Does your pup like to percolate? Well, probably not, but that doesn't mean she doesn't like hanging out with all the other Java junkies at the coffee shop. Most coffee shops have outdoor patio areas where dogs are allowed as long as they are leashed and well behaved. It's become accepted at our local coffee shop for patrons to bring their pups. It always sparks conversations with others and is good socialization for you and your dog, too. If you enjoy going out for a cup of coffee, why not take your best friend along with you? She'll love all the attention she gets from everyone.

My basset hound, Bubba, loves to go with me to the coffee shop. We sit on the patio out in front of the shop and while I'm sipping my cup of caffeine, he gets to meet other people and their dogs. He loves the attention from passersby who stop to pet him and fuss over him. So far he hasn't expressed a desire for an espresso, but it's probably only a matter of time before he's slinging java as well as slobber from his pendulous jowls.

 Puddle Wading

Remember how you loved wading in puddles when you were a child? What could be more fun than stomping and splashing through a big puddle in your rubber boots? Why, stomping through puddles with your dog, of course! You can even buy rubber booties and a raincoat for him to wear on a rainy day, although he probably won't want his friends to see him in that get-up. These boots are made for splashing, so put on those boots and splash away. Your dog will love it, and so will your inner rainy-day child. If the puddle is muddy, all the better!

 Doggie Dress-up

It's sometimes said that people look like their dogs. These days, you're just as likely to see people and their dogs who not only look alike but also dress alike. What could be more fun than dressing to the nines with your canine? But better hold onto your poochie Gucci! Some of that canine couture and bow-wow bling can be nearly as expensive as that of their humans. There are even fashion shows for dogs and their owners. Doting dog owners don't seem to mind the cost, though, as long as their dog is the best dressed on the block. Apparently, nothing is too good for a fashionable Fido and friend.

 Shop 'til You Bark

Could it be that dogs are becoming as materialistic as their owners? If you've flipped through the pages of *Dogue* or *New York Dog* magazines, the answer to that question might be, "Duh." There are also plenty of upscale Bow-wow-tiques for browsing with Bowser. Knowing the credit card companies, your dog might even have received a credit card in the mail with his name on it. If you were born to shop, then shopping might also be your dog's thing. For instance, Wendy Kowalewsky's dog, Chelsea, is definitely a material girl. She loves to go shopping at the pet store. Wendy leads her up and down the aisles and lets Chelsea pick out her own toys. If your dog gets her own credit card, she may just shop 'til she barks!

Lap Dog

If you have a swimming pool, you probably enjoy swimming a few laps each day. Why not invite your dog to join you? It's good exercise for you and also for her. If you happen to have a Labrador or a golden retriever, she probably won't need much coaxing to go a few laps with you. In fact, she'll probably already be in there, dog-paddling away. If your dog isn't such a good swimmer, you can always buy her a life vest so she can still be a lap dog.

Pickpocket Pup

If you have an artful dodger in your house who is always nosing into things and looking for an easy mark, here's something to try that will give him some fun and some practice at being a master pickpocket. Hide some treats in your pockets. The more pockets in the clothes you wear for this game, the better. Better not wear your Sunday best, though. Not only will your little Oliver have a great time learning to pick your pockets for a reward, but you'll also keep the little Dickens entertained for a while.

Stare Wars

The Jack Russell terrier Eddie in the TV series *Frasier* was a master at this game, and so are most dogs, especially if there's food involved. You've probably noticed yours staring at you when you're sitting at the dinner table or eating something he's hoping you'll share. Well, how about turning the tables? Like Frasier, you can stare back at your dog. Try it and see who blinks first. You can even try smiling at your dog. You never know, he might just smile back at you.

Leapdog

If you've ever played leapfrog, then you already know how to play leapdog. The only difference is that your dog is the one doing the leaping. Get down on all fours. This is usually enough to encourage most dogs to play with you, since they just love it when you come down to their level. If she doesn't get the idea right away, you can train your dog to leap over your back. Pat the floor or hold a treat in one hand to coax her over to the other side. Repeat the command, "Leap," a few times and reward her, and she'll soon find this froggy-inspired game absolutely ribbeting.

 Follow the Leader

Here's a simple game to play with your dog that you no doubt played as a child. It involves no special setup, although having a dog that comes when called is helpful. If not, you can always entice him to follow you with a yummy treat. When I was young I loved playing follow the leader with my dog, Dusty. Sometimes he followed me, and sometimes I followed him, on all fours. Just like in Washington, D.C., it doesn't much matter who's doing the leading as long as there's someone who is willing to follow you anywhere.

 Whine and Cheese Tasting

My dogs just love cheese, and whenever I sit down to eat some cheese with my wine, I know I'm going to have to share. So I slice off a few slivers for them, too. Occasionally, I make an event out of it and bring out several different kinds of cheese. Forget about the stinky Limburger and sharp Stilton, though. Like me, they prefer to sample a nice aged cheddar or a creamy Brie or Havarti. Whenever I hear the familiar whine, I know it's time to slice off another piece. Sometimes I have to make the dogs wait their turn, though, because I serve no whine before its time. While cheese in large quantities is not recommended by veterinarians, an occasional sample of cheese won't harm your dog—French poodle or otherwise.

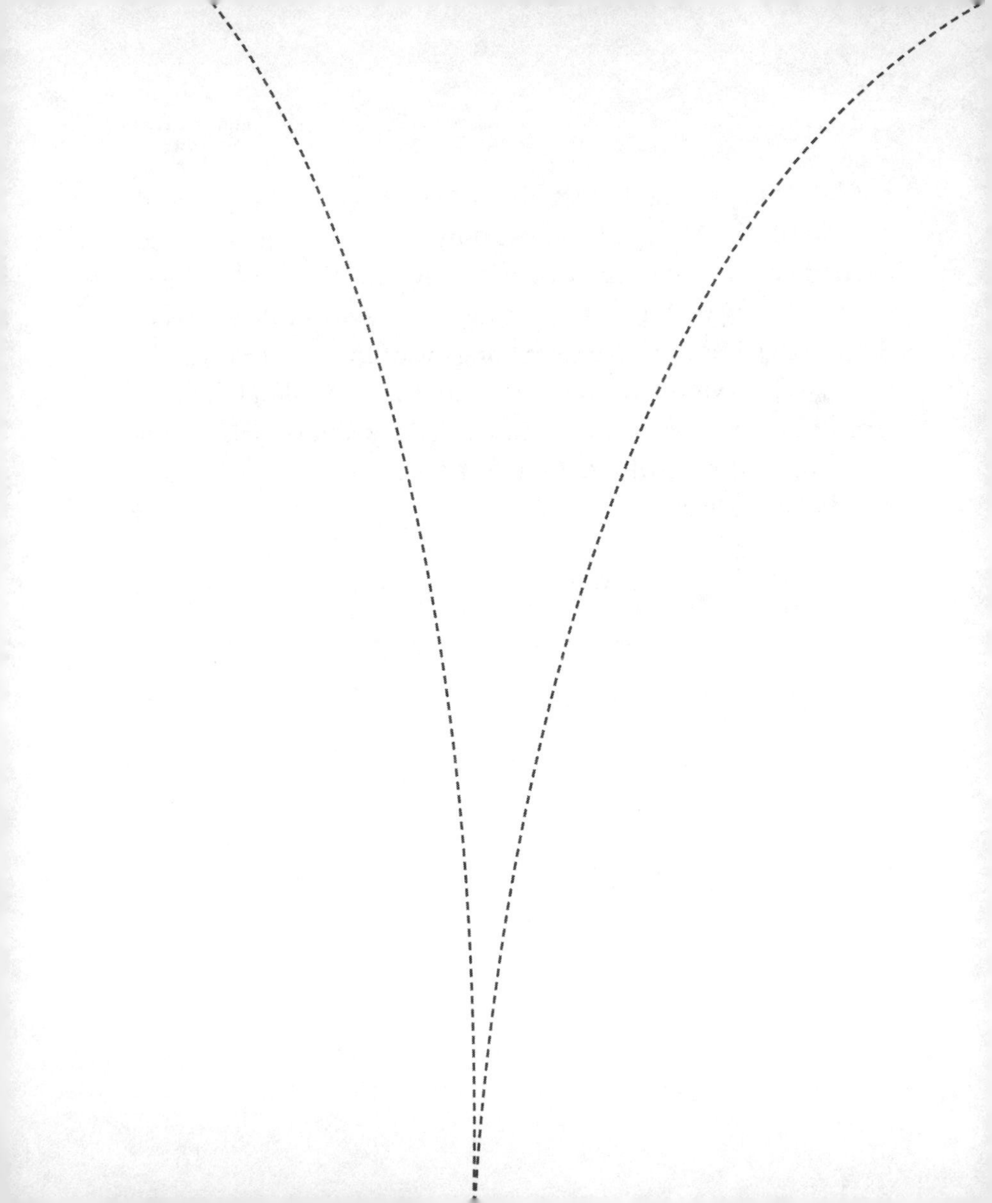

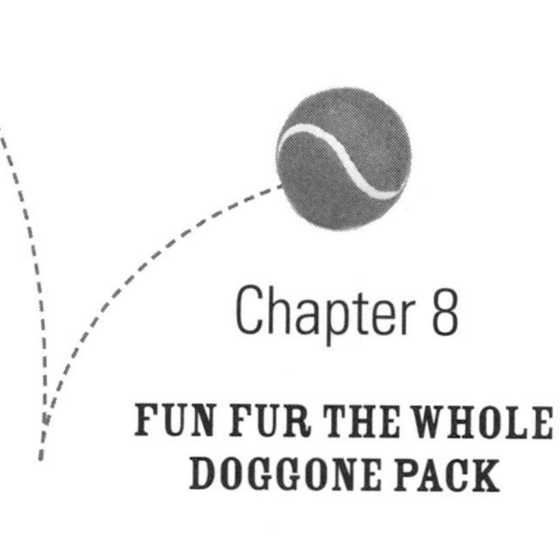

Chapter 8

FUN FUR THE WHOLE DOGGONE PACK

When it comes to dogs having fun, the more the merrier. Just ask any dog and he'd probably agree. Dogs are by nature more content when hanging with the pack. In the wild, canids live in a cooperative, hierarchical society that ensures their survival and the survival of their progeny. It's no different for your dog. Even though dogs no longer need to hunt in packs to survive, they are still happier when in the presence of their own kind. Anyone who's watched a litter of puppies playing and engaging in mock battles or a bunch of dogs cavorting together at an off-leash park knows this to be true. In this final chapter, I suggest some activities that are intended to entertain your bored, domesticated canine and his compadres, too.

Bark in the Park

At the top of the fun-for-Fido-and-his-friends list is the dog park. Nearly every urban area offers at least one off-leash dog park for its canine citizens to engage in a little unfettered socialization with their own kind. Some cities offer more of these dog-friendly spaces than others, and the sizes of the areas vary widely. In Sacramento, California, a group called Sacramento Dog Owners Group (SacDOG) has lobbied the Parks and Recreation District for years to persuade them to designate an off-leash area along the American River parkway. This is a beautiful nature area that includes hiking, biking, and equestrian trails but until recently had no area where dogs were allowed without a leash. That left dog owners wondering, what about the dogs? Dogs just want to have fun, too!

SacDOG eventually succeeded in securing seventy-five acres of off-leash area for Sacramento dogs and their owners to enjoy. This advocacy group for dog lovers was formed in 2002 at a time when frustrated owners were being cited repeatedly for allowing their dogs to run loose along the riverbanks. Having been a dog owner who has lived along this parkway since 1967, I include myself in that group. Now it will be legal to let dogs take a dip in the river and frolic on the sandy banks without fear of being cited by the pooch police. If you have an off-leash area in your community, by all means let your dog bark in the park, but remember you are your own best advocate for more Fido freedom. Always be sure to observe proper dog park etiquette.

Fun-Raisers

There's no limit to the number of ways people and their dogs can gather together to raise funds to benefit animal rescue organizations. Many community shelters host Dog Walk-a-thons or Doggie Dashes where people collect pledges or pay an entry fee to participate in the event. It's a great way to exercise your dog and let her socialize with other dogs, but it's also pretty good exercise for the two-leggers. Even better, it helps raise money for homeless pets. No matter who crosses the finish line first, it's win-win for all.

Host a Pup Picnic

For a number of years I hosted a basset hound picnic every July 14, which is Bastille Day in France, where the basset originated. It so happened that when we moved into our neighborhood back in the 1970s, there were seven basset hounds living in the area. I decided it would be fun for all of them to get together for a picnic, so I invited all the owners and their dogs to a local park for the First Annual Basset Hound Picnic.

Here is part of a poem I wrote about our annual event:

The Annual Basset Hound Picnic
On Bastille Day in July of each year
Basset hounds gather from far and near;
One by one and in pairs they appear
At the annual basset hound picnic.
Hounds of every size and color
Seem genuinely glad to see one another;
Some even greet a sister or brother
At the annual basset hound picnic.
There's Noodles, Cruiser, Patti, and Maggie,
Alex and Dolly with the tail so waggy;
All of their suits are a little too baggy
At the annual basset hound picnic.
After the howl-off and race, they all nap
On a comfy blanket or somebody's lap
Drifting to Dreamland is always a snap
At the annual basset hound picnic.
When finally it's time to say, "Adieu,"

One by one, or two by two,
Everyone says, "We'll be seeing you
At next year's basset hound picnic."

After our first event the word got around, and in subsequent years more dogs and their owners joined the group. Some even brought rescue dogs that were adopted at the event. It was hard to tell who had more fun, the dogs or the people. You can host your own picnic for friends and their pets with games, contests, and food. Of course, picnickers should be prepared to share the contents of their picnic baskets with the dogs. If it's a basset hound picnic like we had, though, those notorious mooches will probably just help themselves to whatever they want.

Here is just one of many fun activities to include when hosting your own picnic.

Doggie Dash

On your marks, get set, dash! A popular event at many dog gatherings is a race to see who has the speediest dog. All you need is an area with enough space to stage a race. It helps if you work in pairs, with someone to restrain the dog at the starting line and someone at the finish line to summon the dog. And you'll need someone impartial to judge the winner. If you have a swift breed like a greyhound or whippet, he may need a handicap, and there could be a photo finish. There's probably no chance of that with basset hounds, though. In fact, extra incentive may be required for these scent hounds to complete the race. Food is an enticement, but don't be disappointed if your dog becomes distracted by a hot scent along the way and doesn't cross the finish line at all.

Yappy Happy Hour

Unlike in English pubs, where dogs are welcomed and often share a pint with their owners, dogs still can't have a bark tab at most American watering holes. Until that day comes (and it may not be too far in the future, as dogs become more widely accepted at social gatherings) you can host your own Yappy Happy Hour at your home, a park, or other Fido-friendly location. The Days Inn in Morris, Illinois, welcomes people and their dogs in town for the annual Basset Waddle in nearby Dwight. Hotels like this one might host a happy hour for the hounds in their conference room, where treats and refreshments are served for their two-legged and four-legged guests.

Bark-B-Q

When you're planning your next backyard barbeque, why not invite a few of the neighborhood folks and their dogs to join you and your dog in a canine cookout? You can barbeque steaks, chicken, and the usual favorites, hamburgers and hot dogs. Dogs aren't fussy, but they don't much care for condiments like mustard and ketchup. If you're serving hamburgers or dogs to the dogs, by all means, hold the onions. Onions are not safe for dogs to eat. Actually, you can hold everything but the meat.

Mutt's Mad Hatter Tea Party

"I'm late, I'm late, for a very important date." The white rabbit in *Alice and Wonderland* knew he mustn't be late for the Mad Hatter's tea party, but he might be surprised to see who turns up at this one. All the guests at this tea party will be dogs, and they'll be sporting hats of all kinds. So will their owners. The dogs probably won't care much for sipping tea, although I once had a dog that enjoyed drinking tea from a saucer. Patience didn't care for lemon or sugar, but she loved milk in her tea, English style. These mad hatters will love sampling the biscuits and dainties you serve from the local dog bakery. But you may want them to skip any cookies that say, “Eat me.”

Basset Waddle

After the publication of my first dog-lover’s mystery, *Howling Bloody Murder,* I was invited to attend the Illinois Basset Waddle, held every year in Dwight, Illinois, to benefit Guardian Angel Basset Rescue. When I attended the Waddle in September of 2002, the highlight of the event for me was the Basset Bash. Besides the silent auction, the barbeque, and the wide assortment of booths selling all manner of basset lover’s wares, the event included various contests in which the dogs competed for prizes. It’s best to choose several people to judge the contest so that no one can be accused of showing favoritism toward their own fur kid. Find out more about the Illinois Basset Waddle and Guardian Angel Basset Rescue at *www.bassetrescue.org.* Other basset rescue organizations throughout the country also host waddles, slobberfests, and drool-a-paloozas.

The Howl-Off

If you've never been within earshot of a howling contest, as I have, you'd probably agree that you've never heard sweeter—or louder—music. Your own dog may be a pup Pavarotti just waiting to be discovered. Some vocally gifted dogs have even appeared on television. You may have to coax your dog to express his singing ability by making some pretty strange sounds of your own. To get our first basset, Butterscotch, to howl, we had to gobble like a turkey. Some people play a musical instrument like a horn or harmonica to get their dogs to join in. If you have your own howl-off, the greatest challenge in this tonsil-busting contest may be in judging who are the best vocalists, the humans or the hounds.

Best Trick

Another judging contest you can stage at your event is "best trick." Some dogs can do some pretty amazing feats. I've seen dogs dispense their own treats, do acrobatics, and even paint pictures! The kinds of tricks are limited only by the imagination of the owner and willingness of the dog to perform them on command.

 Best Treat Catch

This is a contest any dog will gladly compete in, although some may be more adept at intercepting the pitch than others. You can use an overhand or underhand style to toss the treat. Or you can get jiggy with it and do some fancy pitches to impress the judges. The dog probably won't care how you toss the treat, just as long as you don't fake him out and make him think you tossed the treat when you are still palming it. Baseball batters and dogs just hate that!

 Dogtoberfest

Autumn is a great time of year to host a different kind of dog gathering I like to call Dogtoberfest. After several years of hosting the basset hound picnic in July, I decided that for the sake of our bassets, which don't tolerate summer heat as well as some breeds do, autumn might be a better time of year to throw our annual pup party. So on October 1, all the dogs and their owners gathered at our nearby park for the festivities. We had German music, food, and games for the people and their dogs. Next autumn, you might like to host your own Dogtoberfest. Dirndls and lederhosen are optional.

 Doggie Smorgasbord

If your dog is a chowhound, he won't be bored at a smorgasbord just for dogs. For your bowser buffet, you can include various kinds of treats the dogs will love. You can offer safe and healthy food choices as well as decadent delicacies you purchase from your local dog bakery or make at home. Everyone can contribute his or her own special recipe, and there are plenty these days to try. Cookbooks for canines abound at bookstores and pet shops. You can place the food on the floor for smaller dogs to access or on a dining table for the benefit of the expert counter surfers in the group.

 Wiener Dog Race

The highlight of the Dogtoberfest was the wiener dog race. No, I don't mean that wiener dogs were racing, although if you have wiener dogs, you can certainly race them. In this event, the dogs were racing after the wieners. The owners ran out in front of their basset hounds with a hot dog lure to coax the dogs to run. It didn't take much for the dogs to engage in the polska kiel*basset* pursuit. Our sides were splitting with laughter as we watched the dogs pursue the dogs. The humans got some good exercise, too, in this hot dog heat. At the end of the race, it was wiener take all!

Frisbee Fling

Frisbee tossing isn't just fun for two but has been elevated to a competitive national sport. If there were dog Olympics, the Frisbee toss no doubt would be one of the main events. You've probably seen these competitions on Animal Planet and other pet shows. If so, you know that you'll never see a dog acting bored as long as he's engaged in a lively game of Fetch the Frisbee. Some of the dogs leap so high you expect them to sprout wings and fly.

It's even more fun when done with a group of other dogs and their owners. You don't necessarily have to enter a competition, unless you want to, of course. Until you and your dog have perfected your technique for the nationals, you can always host your own fun Frisbee toss in your backyard or at a neighborhood park for your friends and their dogs. Everyone is sure to have a fling with the Frisbees.

 Pawjama Party

If you and your dog are in the mood for a little pillow talk, why not invite the whole gang and their dogs over for a pajama party? The dogs can come as they are, or dress in PJs, like their owners. Pop some popcorn for the people, provide some Pup-peroni for the dogs, and a fun night is guaranteed for everyone. What's a slumber party without some movies to watch from dusk to dawn? Since this is a pup pajama party, you can choose from a whole litter of great dog movies. For laughs, there's *The Shaggy Dog* or *Beethoven*, or you can rent ten-tissue classics like *Where the Red Fern Grows* or *Lassie, Come Home*. Or if you're into scary mutt movies and the dogs aren't too squeamish, you can always rent *Cujo* or *Pet Sematary*. You'd better skip showing *They Only Kill Their Masters*, though, since you're making the dogs wear those silly-looking dog PJs in front of their buddies. They might decide to gang up on you.

 Campfire Grrrls

Pitching a pup tent takes on a whole new meaning when you take your dog to one of the many dog camps that have sprung up across the country. For instance, located on the shore of beautiful Lake Tahoe in the Sierra Nevada Mountains, Camp Winnaribbun provides thirty-three acres of fragrant pine forest for you and your dog to explore, as well as private beachfront so you both can frolic in the clear, blue waters of one of the most beautiful lakes in the country.

Camp W offers campers the opportunity to participate in obedience, agility, herding, tracking, flyball, games, crafts, and photo sessions. It also offers health services such as homeopathy, psychocybernetics, and massage therapy. Campers and their dogs sleep in rustic cabins after a busy day of nature hikes, arts and crafts, S'mores and, finally, storytelling around a roaring campfire. What better getaway for your dog and his best friend?

 Howloween Costume Party

Occasionally, while doing book signings at local pets shops in the fall, I've been asked to judge a Howloween costume contest. Choosing the best costume award winner is always a challenge with so many cleverly dressed contenders. There was an Afghan hound dressed in an *I Dream of Genie* costume. One dog owner came disguised in a silver astronaut space suit and paraded around the judging ring with her trio of Yorkshire terriers, which masqueraded as extraterrier-estrials. This contest inspired a chapter in my second dog lover's mystery novel, *Sirius About Murder*.

The most hilarious costume I ever saw was one of the dogs at the Illinois Basset Waddle, where I saw a Basset Boeing 747. No, they didn't use the dog's ears for wings. The basset wore a body stocking with the plane's wings fastened to it. Everyone at the fall event was howling, including the dogs.

You can host your own contest and offer prizes for the entrants. Entry fees are optional for the contest, but this can also be a great way to raise funds to be donated to animal rescue. You can also take the dogs out Halloween night for bark-or-treat at prearranged dog-friendly houses.

 Maypole Dog Dance

Ah, spring! The time for blossoming flowers and dancing around the maypole, but this ancient German pagan tradition isn't just for people. Dogs can also join in this colorful fun on the first day of May. Just attach the colorful ribbons to your dog's collar and lead him around the maypole with the other dogs. Weaving in and out with the other dog walkers and their pets will plait the ribbons in a multicolored pattern on the pole. Walking the dogs in the reverse direction will unbraid the ribbons and rebraid them. It's fun to see if you can braid the ribbons without getting them tangled. Dancing is optional, but if you do you might find that your dog will enjoy dancing along with you. Just don't let the dogs piddle on the maypole, and be careful that none of the dogs gets caught up in the ribbons.

Canine Carnival

There may not yet be a Six Wags theme park for dogs, but you can always have your own canine carnival in the backyard or at a local dog-friendly park. Again, this activity can serve as a fundraiser for dog rescue. You could offer waggin' train rides in a converted Radio Flyer kid's wagon or a trailer pulled behind a bicycle. There could be a dunking booth for the water dogs and their owners. What a great way for everyone to cool off on a hot day! Of course, as is the case at any carnival, there should be lots of yummy treats available to eat, for the dogs as well as the people. And don't forget the sideshow barker!

Pup Piñata Party

The Chihuahua and Tepeizeuintli—yes, it's a dog, better known as the Mexican hairless—will appreciate this activity for a canine Cinco de Mayo celebration. Next May 5, invite your friends and their dogs for a Fido fiesta and watch the fun unfold like a matador's cape. For this event, you'll need a piñata, of course, filled with a bounty of treats for the dogs. If the piñata is shaped like a dog, even better. It will be fun for the owners to try to break the piñata open in the traditional way, blindfolded, with a stick. Or you can always just let the dogs tear into it. After they finish off the piñata and goodies inside, they'll no doubt be ready for their siesta.

Carol of the Barks

On the twelfth day of Christmas, all the dogs will be barking a Christmas carol when you join with your friends and their merry caroling canines for a stroll through the neighborhood next season. If the weather outside is frightful, don't forget sweaters or coats and snow boots for the dogs.

Of course, residents who can fully appreciate this rather unusual seasonal serenade will be expected to have biscuits and dog nog on hand to offer the four-legged carolers. It's probably best to carol at houses where you know there are other dog lovers, or you can send out a flyer beforehand to let people know you'll be coming by to entertain them and wish them happy howlidays.

 Have a Field Day

If you have a dog that was bred specifically for the hunt, there may be a very good reason why she looks so bored with her suburban domestic life. When it comes to hunting dogs, you can take the dog out of the field, but you can't take the field out of the dog. You would be amazed at the dramatic transformation in that sofa warmer of yours when you take her to her first field trial. Here she can match her sniffing or pointing skills against others of her kind in the hunt.

Some training probably will be required before you participate in your first trial, but seeing dogs doing what they were bred to do is as much a joy for their owners as it is for the dogs. Besides being a wonderful outing for you and your dog, this is an exercise in obedience and tracking skills. Whether your dog's instinct is for tracking rabbits, as is the case with basset hounds, or flushing a covey of quail as do pointers and setters (unless Dead-eye Dick Cheney has spotted them first), she's always at the ready when you cry, "Tally-ho!"

 Tailwagger's Wedding

Here comes the bride, all dressed in white, from her head to all four feet. At this wedding, the bride and groom won't exchange vows but bow-wows, the cake will have canines on the top, and the wedding party may look a bit unusual, too. It's no secret that people have gone a little nuts over their dogs. There are no lengths to which we won't go to make our dogs happy, or at least what we think will make them happy. These days when boy dog meets girl dog, you can make it an affair to remember. There may not yet be a *Dog Bride* magazine, but magazines like *Hollywood Dog* and *New York Dog* regularly feature fancy apparel for just such occasions. The bride will be stunning in her satin dress and veil, complemented by her bridesmaids in chiffon. Jewelry by Tiffany. Of course, the groom and best man will be dressed in tie and tails. Don't forget to have a photographer present to capture the event for the four-leggers' heirloom family album. Wedding gifts are fine, too, but you might want to skip getting this bride and groom a toaster. As for the honeymoon, a night of romance at a five-bone hotel is probably just the ticket.

Bowser Bridal Shower

What's a wedding without a shower for the bride? Before the big event, you can have a lot of fun throwing a shower for the canine bride-to-be. Invite your friends and their dogs—girls only allowed, of course, unless you decide to bring in the Chippendogs to entertain the group. For the dogs, make up some party favor bags filled with scrumptious treats. Shower gifts could include gag gifts or items for the couple to set up housekeeping in their new doghouse—his and hers dog bowls, a king-size dog bed, you get the picture. And what would any shower be without a few party games and prizes?

Puppy Bump Shower

First comes love, then comes marriage, then comes the litter of puppies in a baby carriage. After the bridal shower and wedding naturally comes the mutt maternity shower, unless the newlyweds decide to practice birth control (better known as spay and neuter), which we all know is the responsible thing to do to control pet overpopulation. Besides, it would probably be too much to expect your friends to buy eight of everything for this expectant mother. That would be thirty-two booties to knit!

 Scavenger Hunt

What better activity for animals that descended from scavengers than a scavenger hunt? You may have taken part in a scavenger hunt before. It's a fun and energetic team activity in which participants seek to find all the items on a list or complete certain tasks. In this doggie scavenger hunt, you could include things on your list that your dog can help you find, such as a bone, a ball, or a rawhide chew. Of course, if your dog is anything like mine, she might be more interested in seeking a cat or a squirrel, if those items happen to be on your list.

 Skateboard Race

You've probably seen kids in your neighborhood on skateboards being towed by their dogs. The dogs always seem to be having a swell time, and so are the kids. Get several dogs pulling their owners on a skateboard and you have the makings of a great race. It doesn't have to be a marathon, just a short dash. Be sure to match the size of the dog to the amount of weight he's pulling on the skateboard. If you have a draft dog, which is accustomed to pulling more weight than the average dog, all the better. The closer the match between racers, the fairer the race, but it's all in fun. You're not competing in the Canine Olympics, after all.

Note: This can also be done on in-line skates.

Barkleys of Broadway

If your dog is always acting up, perhaps it's because he's a Wishbone wannabe just hoping for his big break on the stage. You can help your little ham have some fun by hosting a play for your dog and his performing pals. Costuming the dogs for their parts and reading their lines for them is also a lot of fun for the stage moms and dads. Of course, some dogs may prefer to bark their own parts in the play. You might even like to try writing your own script for this canine acting company. You can even charge admission to the performance and donate the proceeds to animal rescue. Who knows? Your hound could soon be Broadway bound. I hear they're always looking for Sandy understudies in *Annie*.

 Dogue's Gallery

Dog art (and yes, even cat art) is becoming immensely popular among animal lovers and is even pulling prices to rival those works of human artists. Animal welfare organizations are putting to good use the talents of their tailwaggers to raise money to support rescue groups and shelters. You can host your own dog art show to benefit your "pet" cause. In some towns, these events are held in conjunction with monthly citywide tours of art galleries, which draw more people and thereby raise more money. While none of these artworks has yet been auctioned at Christie's, you might just discover you have the next Pablo Pawcasso right in your own backyard.

 Dog Wash

Here's a great way to cool off this summer with your friends and their dogs and also raise some funds for your local animal shelter. Host a community dog wash. Whether he wants it or not, at least once a year your dog needs a bath, even if you're the one who gets most of the dousing. After that last art activity, you both may need a bath. Let's face it, washing the dog is a task most people don't enjoy doing very often.

That's why there are such things as dog grooming salons. A dog wash is a less expensive and more fun way to get a clean canine. You'll need some volunteers who don't mind getting slapped in the face by a wet tail or two.

Barkday Party

Kids aren't the only ones who enjoy having birthday parties. So do the fur kids. A barkday party can be just as much fun for your dog. With so many dog bakeries around these days, you can order a wide variety of treats the dogs will enjoy, such as barkday cakes and pupcakes. Or you can make your own goodies, if you prefer. Add some fun party favors and games for the four-legged partygoers, and an unfurgettable celebration is guaranteed when your dog celebrates her next birthday. She may need some help blowing out the candles, though. Just don't let her pee on them.

Putting on the Dog

Is your dog supermodel material? Is he too sexy for his leash? Could he be a fashion plate for *Dogue* magazine? A fun activity and another great way to raise money for animal rescue is to host a fashion show for dogs. My bassets and I once had the opportunity to participate in one of these events at a local pet shop, which was showcasing its winter clothing line for dogs. Daisy and Bubba were appropriately assigned to the Low-rider Group along with some dachshunds wearing bomber jackets. Most of the dogs were outfitted in colorful sweaters that looked better than mine did and were more expensive. Others wore school-bus-yellow rain slickers with galoshes to match. Bubba also wore a handsome brown, fleece-lined bomber jacket, and Daisy was ready for a snowy Sun Valley weekend in her silver quilted ski jacket with faux fur collar. It was great fun for all, but I'm not sure how the dogs felt about strutting their stuff on a *cat*walk.

Prettiest Dog Contest

If there were a Mister or Miss Dog America contest, would your pet win it paws down? Well, here's your chance to find out. Hold your own dog beauty pageant. This is another event that is great to include at a fundraiser, and the more dogs the merrier. As in Miss America contests, you can have competitions in the best dressed and talent categories (you might want to skip the bathing suit competition), and there is always the crowning ceremony at the finale. Judging who is the fairest fur face of all is purely in fun because everyone naturally thinks his dog is the most beautiful.

Ugliest Dog Contest

If your dog wouldn't stand a Chinese shar pei's chance of winning a prettiest dog contest, maybe he's a contender for the title of ugliest dog now that Sam, once voted the world's ugliest dog, has left that class wide open. Fortunately, with dogs, beauty is only fur deep; they're all beautiful inside. Still, if your dog is so ugly he could stop an eight-day Felix the Cat clock, you could always enter him in an ugly dog contest. It's all in fun, of course, and this is also a popular event at many fundraisers. Offering prizes to the humans and their ugly pets may soothe any hurt feelings, but the dogs don't know or care if they're ugly. They judge everything by how it smells. A human judging the beauty of a dog is purely subjective, though. Luckily for us, dogs don't judge people on their appearance.

Pup Play Date

If you are a member of Generation Y, you probably already know all about play dates, where parents arrange supervised playtimes for their children. Well, Generation Bark is no different. Play dates for your yuppie puppy can be just as much fun for four-legged kids as they are for the two-legged ones. You can also trade off with other pup parents, arranging the play dates around your schedules. Setting up a play date doesn't require anything more special than your time and undivided attention, which is really all your dog ever wants from you, anyway.

Arfs and Crafts

Does your dog have an inner artist just waiting to be discovered? Perhaps she's always wanted a hobby, but you've just never taken the time to find out what kind of hobby she'd like to pursue. Most dogs have a lot of spare time on their paws, and they aren't even retired in most cases. You might be surprised to discover just how talented your dog is. Take the play date a step further and make it more human/dog interactive by introducing various activities, such as paw painting. Your dog could even make a few bucks for you with her arfs and crafts at a craft show. Here are a couple of fun things you can do with the dogs that may also become keepsakes in years to come.

Paws of Clay

Collecting paw prints isn't just for the CSI (Canine Scene Investigation) team. You can make your own imprints of your dog's paws. Some pet stores carry ready-made paw print kits. For more creative fun, you can mold your own paw print plate out of modeling clay, which can be purchased at any art store. Gently press your dog's paw into the moist clay. Don't forget to include the dog's name and the date the paw print was made, which can be traced into the clay with a pointed sculptor's tool. You can paint and fire the clay paw print in a kiln or just leave it au naturel. Before the clay dries, be sure to punch two small holes in the top of the plate so you can thread a ribbon in your special paw print plate for hanging on the wall.

Tailwagger's Tiles

Here's another way to preserve your dog's paw print for posterity. Using nontoxic paint, dip your dog's paw in the paint and press it on plain white kitchen tile. Again, be sure to sign and date the tile. You can either make one to hang on your wall or create a number of them in various colors for tiling in your house. What better doggie décor than these tiles for your tailwagger's room? Or you could intersperse them among the tile work in your kitchen. If your dog is anything like mine, that's where he spends most of his time, anyway.

Pup Pool Party

Splish, splash! Some dogs spend more time in the water than out of it. If you have a dog that loves the water, like a retriever or a duck toller, why not invite all his H_2O-loving pals over for a summer pool party? The dogs will have a blast swimming, splashing, and retrieving whatever you toss into the pool, and they'll stay cool at the same time. So will you when the dogs get out of the pool, shake themselves off, and splatter water all over you. If your dog is not so adept at dog-paddling, you might need to have a lifeguard present.

Splashdown!

Here's some more splashing fun for you and Fido. You may have told some people that you dislike taking a long walk off a short pier, but if you've told your dog to take a long run and leap off the end of that pier, and he actually does it, then you and your dog are definitely into dock diving. The object of this sport is to see how high and how far a dog can leap off of a dock. It's amazing to see how athletic some of the dogs are when participating in a "big air" event. This popular, competitive national sport is obviously for water-loving dogs that don't mind belly flops and enjoy a good splashdown.

In October, 2005, Anna Borovich and her rescue dog, Colby, tied the world record of six feet ten inches in Extreme Vertical at the Cabela's National Dog Diving Championship, as reported on www.dockdogs.com.

Dueling Droolslingers

If you've ever been to a Drool-a-palooza or Jowl-Flappers Fest, which are gatherings held for people and their basset hounds or other breeds with pendulous lips, you know that there's never any shortage of drool at such an event. These folks know how to put all that slobber to good use in a drool-slinging contest, where the dogs flap their lips and the distance the drool flies is measured—sort of a jowl javelin competition. The dog with the farthest fling wins. Just be sure no one is in the line of fire of the jowl-flapper.

Life's a Beach

Dogs are never happier than when frolicking on a beach, feeling the sea spray on their faces and sniffing smelly seaweed or dead fish (and rolling in them). Get several dogs together on the beach, and it's an instant beach party. Your beach party doesn't have to be at the ocean, though. You may live near a lake or a river where there are beaches, too. In our city, we now have a leash-free beach area just for the dogs on the banks of the American River. Whenever you're at a beach anywhere, be sure you observe the local regulations regarding dogs on (or off) the beach, or you could risk a citation from the pooch police.

Rex-treme Dog Sports

Here are a few activities for only the very bravest of dogs.

Surfer Dog Dude

Like people, some dogs may not be content with just your garden-variety backyard activities. Certain breeds of dogs like living life at full speed, and they have the boundless energy to match. You could discover that you're the owner of a dog that prefers to live life on the edge—the edge of a surfboard, that is. If your Moondoggie likes hanging eight and riding the waves, why not share your board with him the next time you shoot the curl? You and your Beach Boy bowser will have a bitchin' time hanging loose on your surfari. Just don't be too surprised if your board buddy does a little hot-dogging of his own while you're shredding that next gangbuster wave.

A Rover Runs Through It

Your water dog may be up for a bit more excitement than just a ho-hum dip in the backyard swimming pool. If that's the case you can take him whitewater rafting, which is guaranteed to be a thrill, not only for him but also for you. You can also do this with a group of people and their dogs for even more fun. Don't forget to wear a lifejacket, and make sure your dog wears one, too. While bucking on the turbulent waters of a wild river is an exciting adventure for you and your dog, you wouldn't want your dog's rafting excursion to end up a Rover of no return.

Cross-Country Skiing

I love to cross-country ski. Besides the fact that it's the best exercise there is, nothing is more soothing to the soul than being out in the silent, snowy woods where the only sounds you hear are a lone stellar jay or clumps of snow dropping from the pine trees. The first time I took my basset hounds along with me to Lake Tahoe in the wintertime, I let them come with me when I skied. Daisy and Bubba raced through the snow and thoroughly enjoyed themselves, even if their bellies did get a little cold; however, I recall they did look rather puzzled at how large Mom's feet had suddenly grown.

Pupeye the Sailor

Here's more fun on a board to keep your dog from being bored. Sailboarding is another sport your dog may take to like a dog takes to water, so to speak. This sport is a little less gonzo than surfing the pipeline, but it's just as much fun. Teach your dog to ride on the nose of the board so he won't be knocked over by the sail's swing. As long as you both wear your life vests and can dog-paddle, you'll be happily sailing into the sunset.

Toboggan for Two (or More)

For some winter fun, there's nothing like frolicking in the snow with your dog. For even more fun, you can take your dog sledding, except he won't be the one pulling—you'll be hauling it up the nearest hill for the two of you to ride down together. If you have a long toboggan, you can invite some of his friends to join you as you shush down the hill. It may not be as thrilling as the Matterhorn ride at Disneyland, but your dog will no doubt think sledding downhill with you is an E-ticket ride.

One of my most joyful childhood memories is of sledding in the snow for the first time with my dog, Dusty. Just a short drive up Highway 50 from the Sacramento Valley rise the majestic Sierra Nevada Mountains, providing a pristine white wonderland in winter and a cool green respite in summer. One winter's day, my dad pulled off the highway at Cisco Grove so I could join the other children who were sledding down a hill. I had no brother or sister then to ride with me on my toboggan, so my best friend, Dusty, rode along with me. We sped down the hill in the sunshine, fresh powder dusting our faces as I held tightly onto Dusty. I don't know which of us had the bigger smile.

Spa Excursion

If you're looking for the perfect getaway with your significant other (the one with four legs and a tail), then here's the perfect finale to all the fun you've been having together—a European spa vacation. Voyages with Dogs is the brainchild of Maria Granata, president of Specialty International Tours. The United States is still playing catch-up to pet-friendly Europe, and Granata was determined to make it possible for Americans to enjoy a relaxing sightseeing tour abroad. Imagine you and your dog taking a leisurely stroll through Strasbourg or touring the wine region in Germany. How about a relaxing stay in the Bavarian Alps or a boat ride on a picturesque alpine lake? It's all part of this fantastic Fido-friendly excursion. You'll have the opportunity to meet and travel with other people and their dogs and visit luxurious pet-friendly European spas. The company offers packages to various destinations abroad that include stays at four-star hotels, transportation, special tours, spa treatments, and every amenity that you and your continental canine will require for a vacation to remember. Just pack the bags and the wags, and you're both on your way.

Unfurgettable Fun

Well, there you have it. You've read about many ways to entertain your dog and keep her from being lonely or bored. Perhaps you can think of some fun ideas of your own that are not included in this book. Keep a record of your own, a Dog Fun Log, in which you can write down what kinds of things your dog enjoys doing, or simply use it to journal about the happy times you spend with your faithful companion. You might also like to keep a scrapbook to paste in photos of your dog having fun by herself, with you, or with the whole doggone pack. That way, you will have a record of your dog's favorite activities to look back on in years to come. You'll smile when you look at the pages and recall all your special times together. You'll also be glad to know that to the best of your ability you always kept your best friend busy and happy.

INDEX

G

H

I

K

ABOUT THE AUTHOR

Sue Owens Wright is the author of The Beanie and Cruiser Dog Lover's Mystery Series and *What's Your Dog's IQ?* Sue is a seven-time nominee and two-time winner of the Maxwell Award by the Dog Writers' Association of America. She and her husband reside in Sacramento, California, with their basset hound.